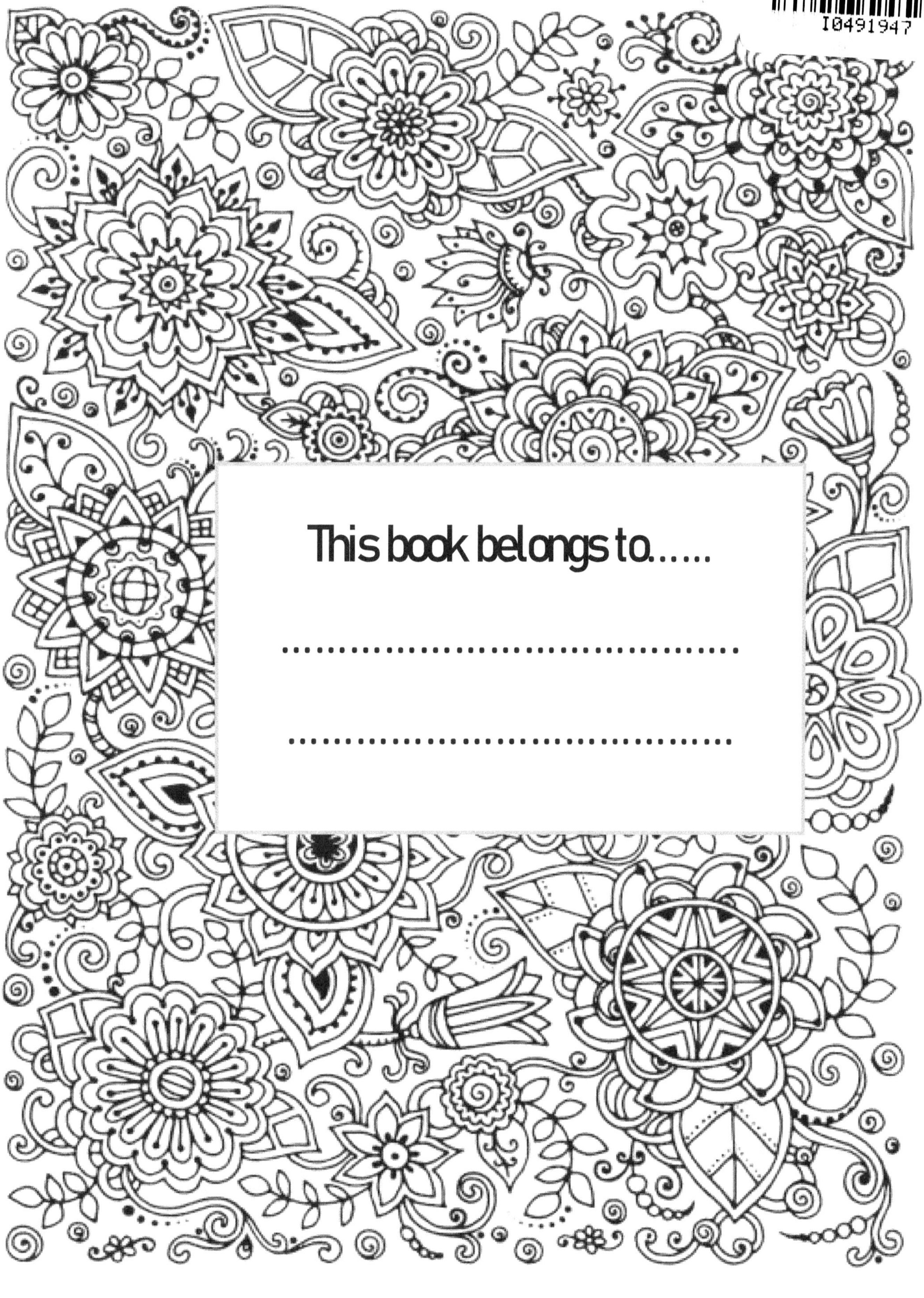

This book belongs to......

....

....

Small preview of what's inside

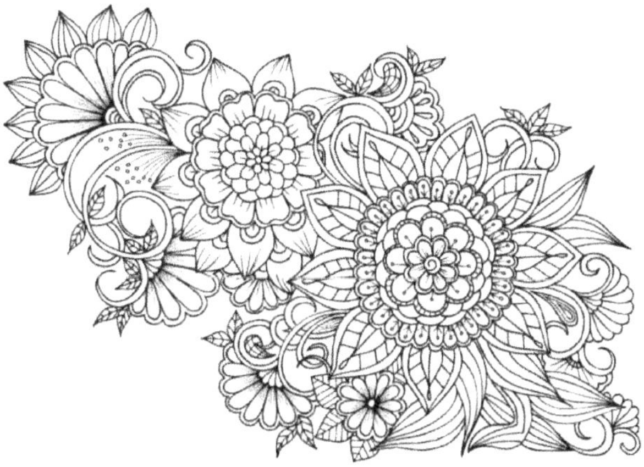

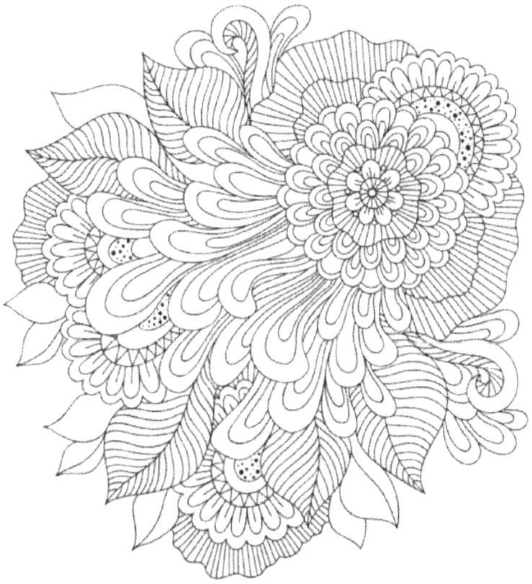

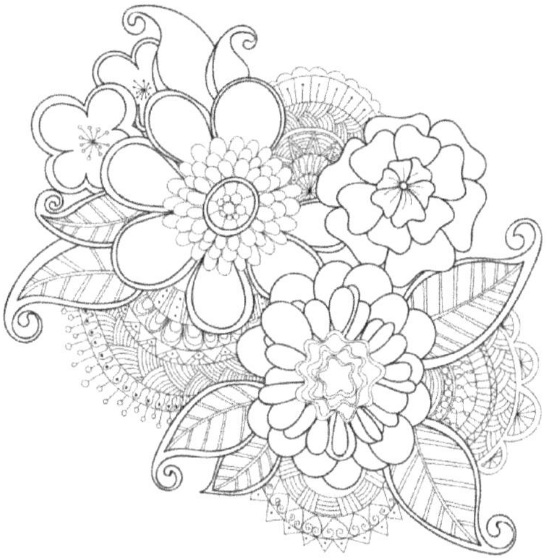

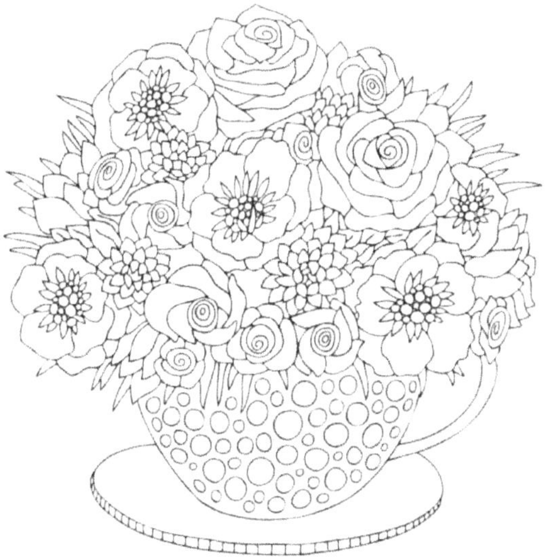

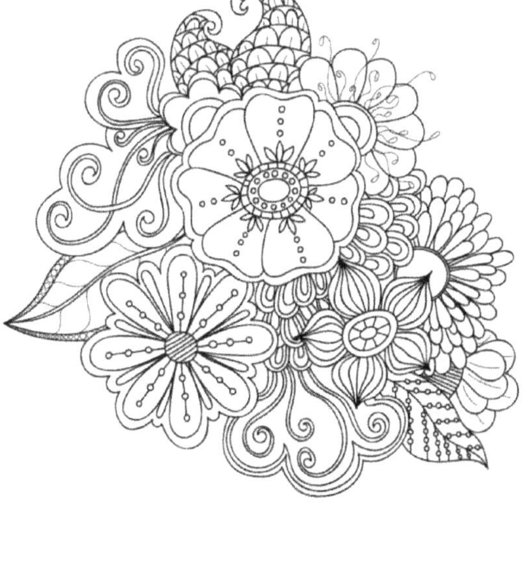

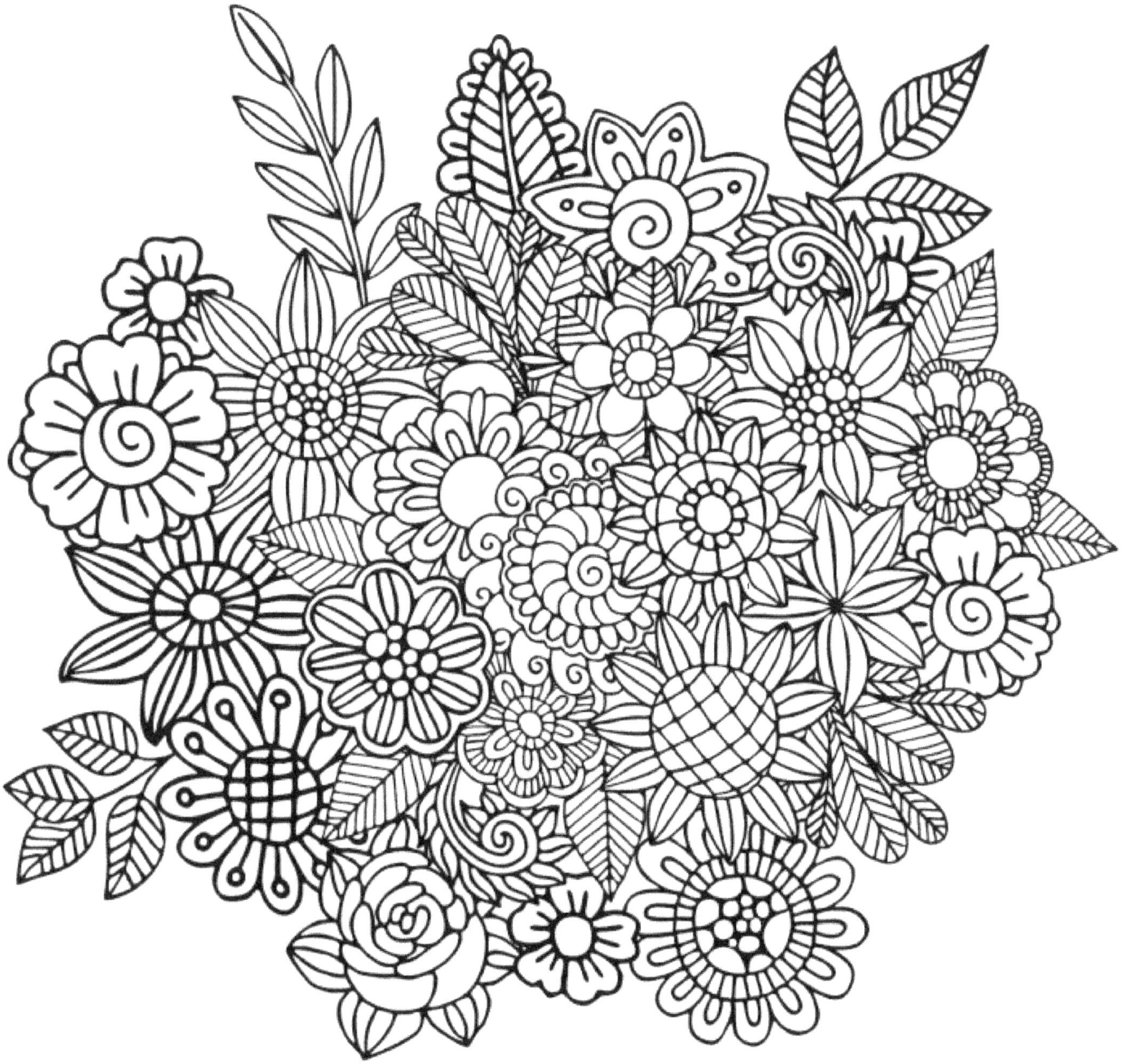

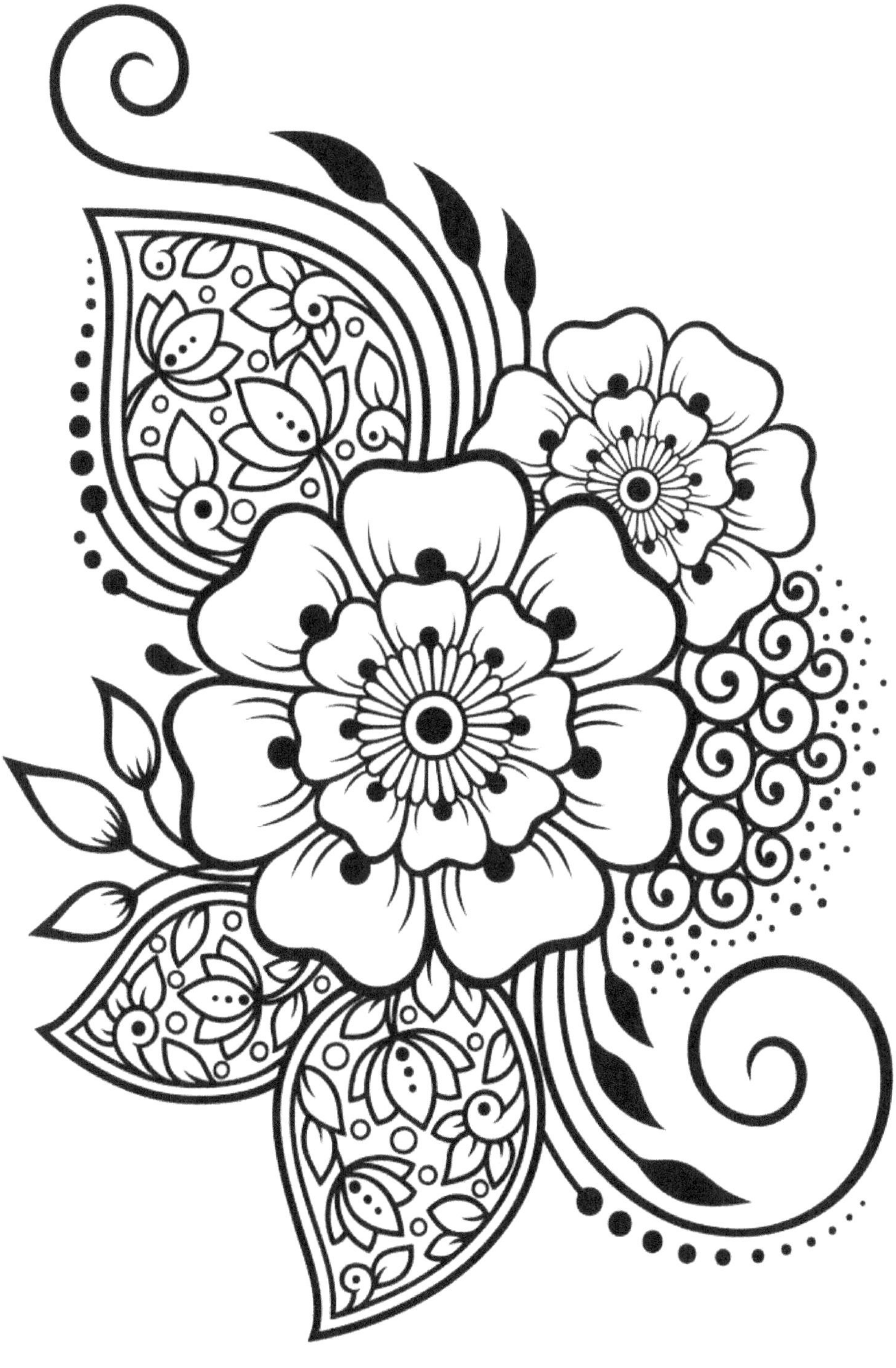

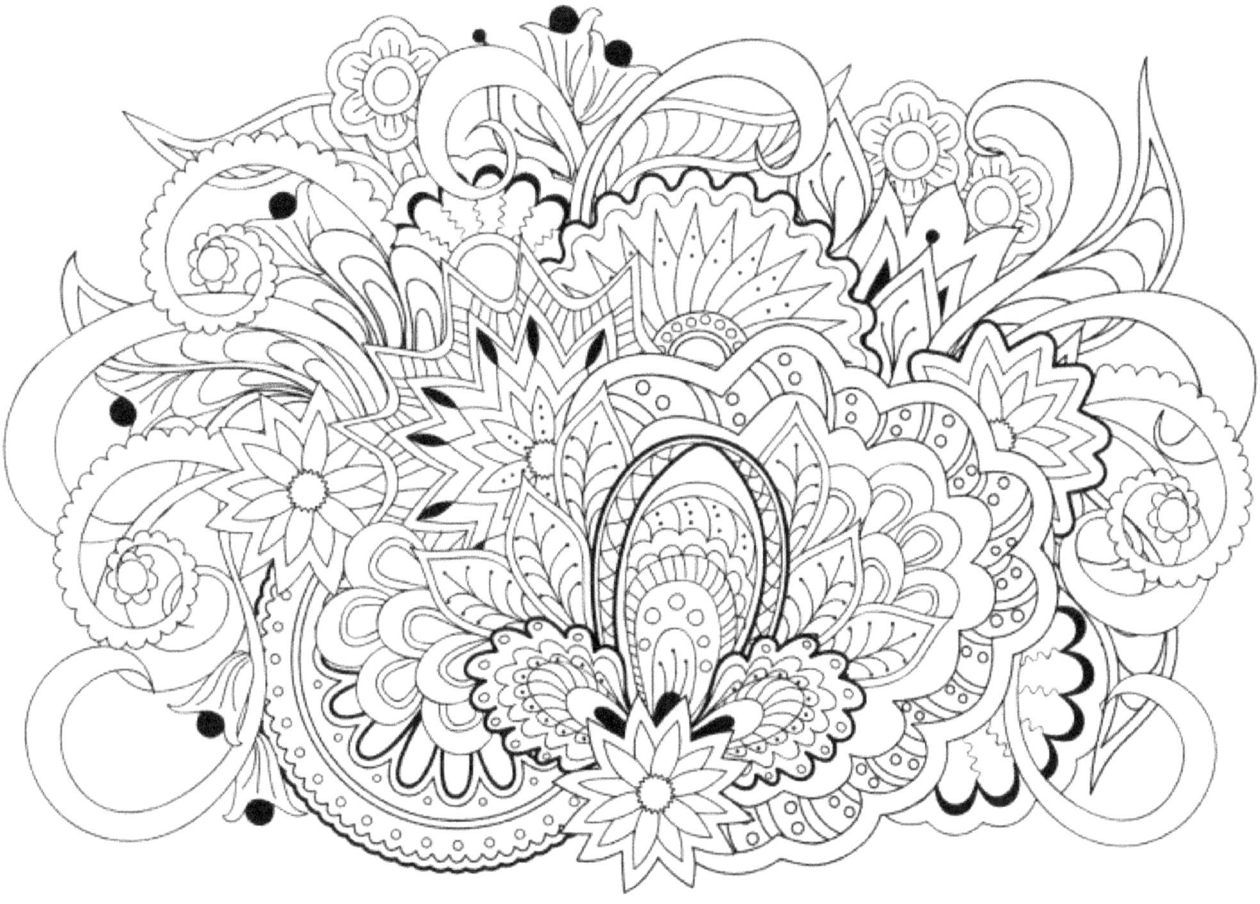

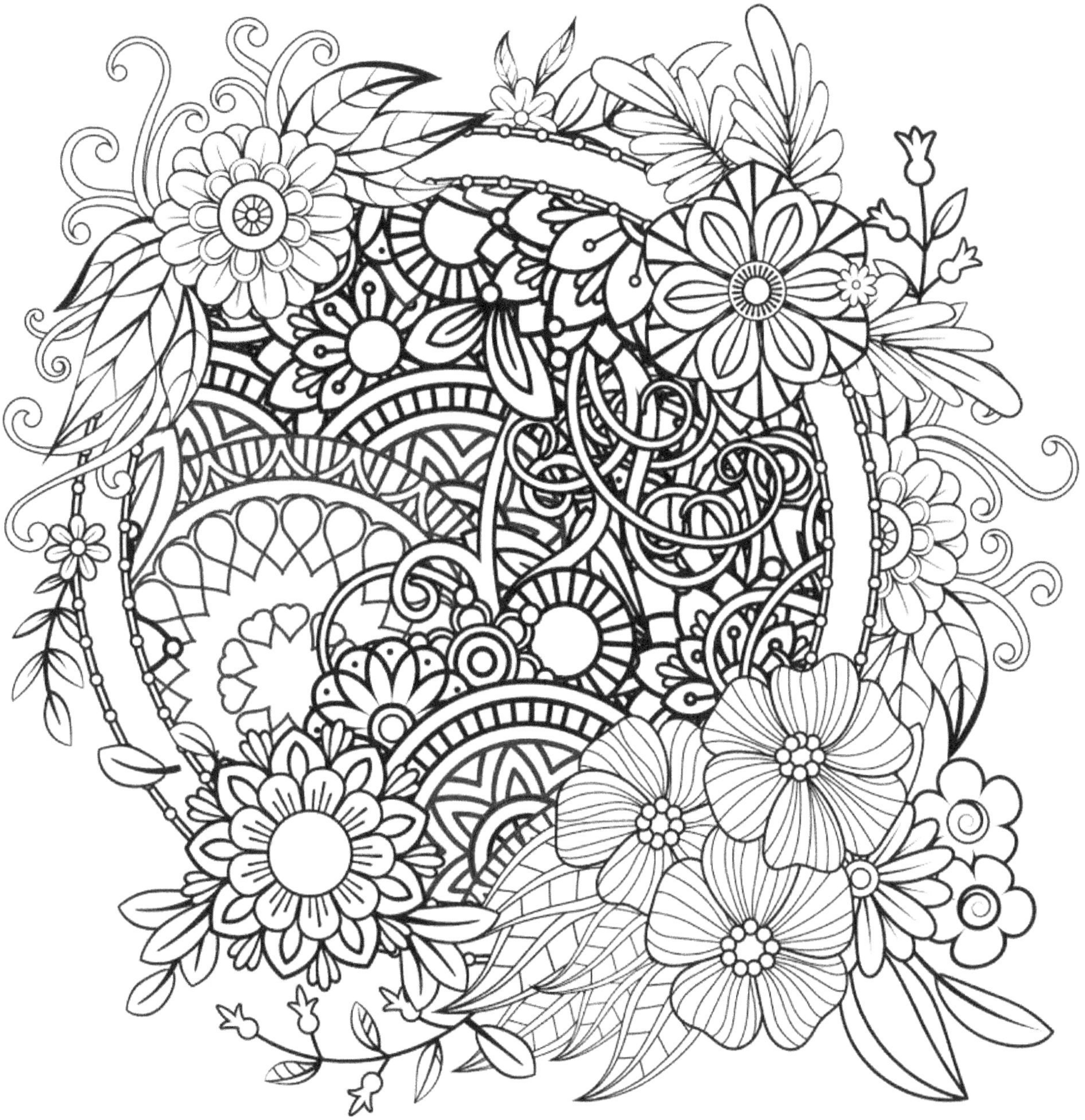

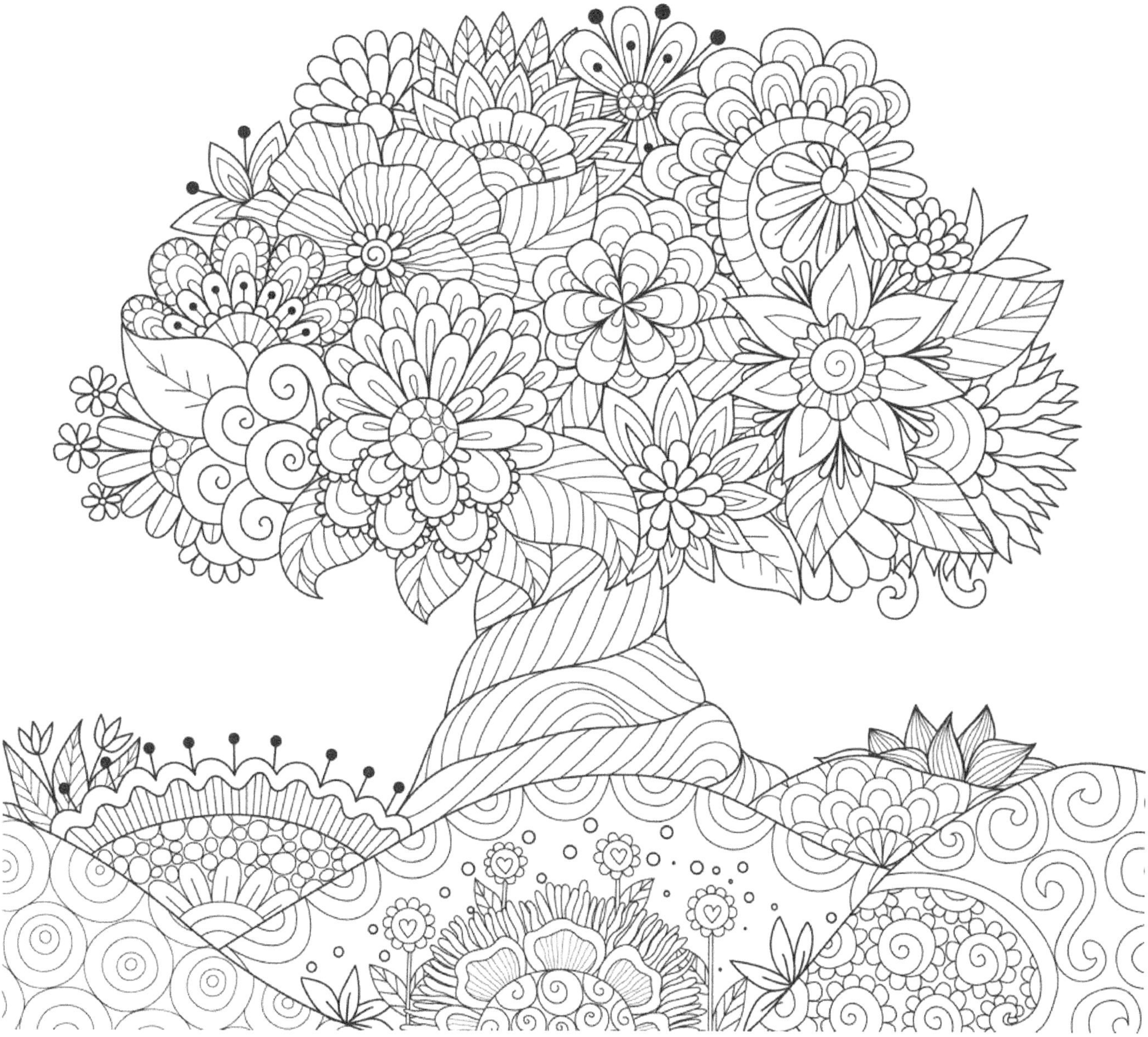

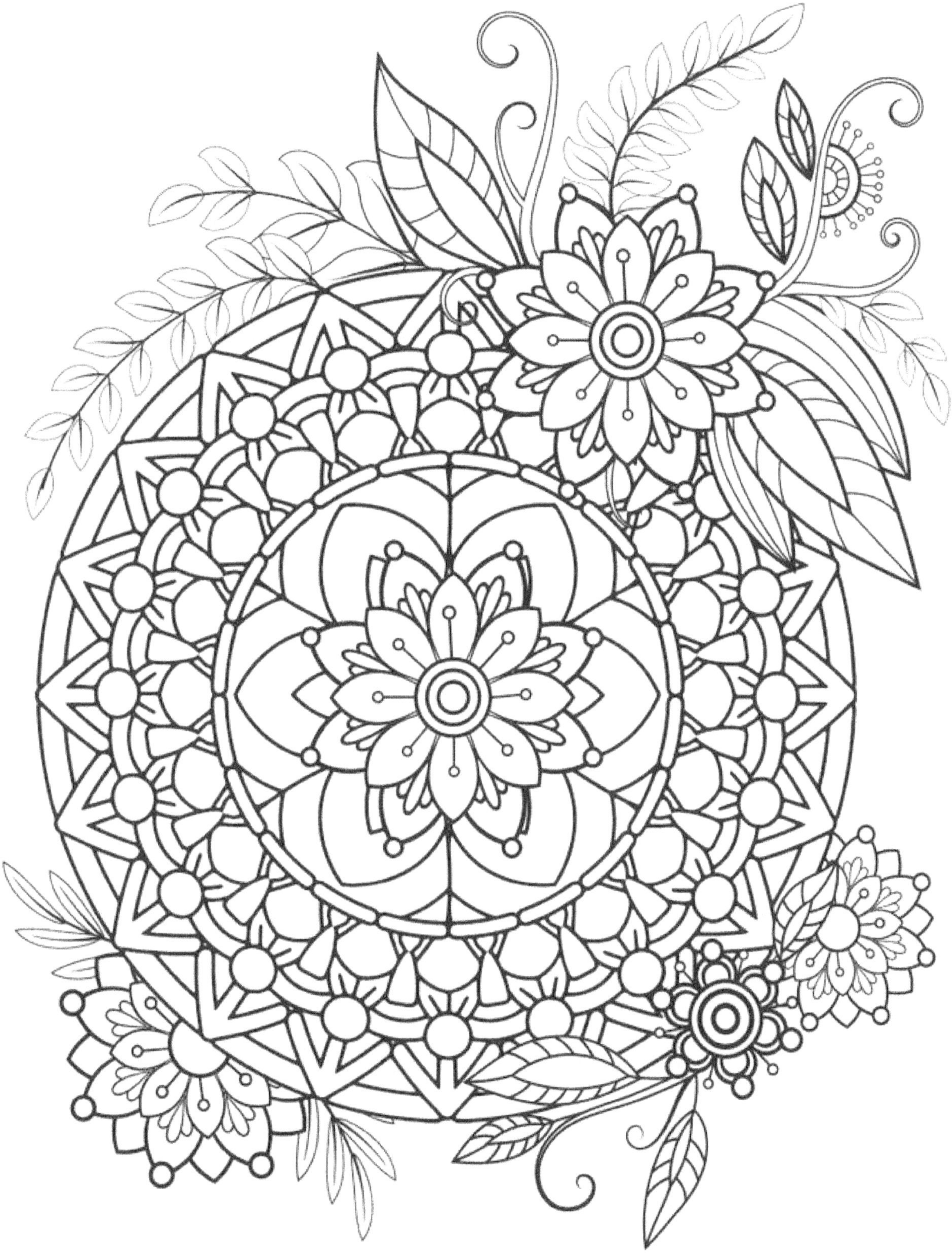

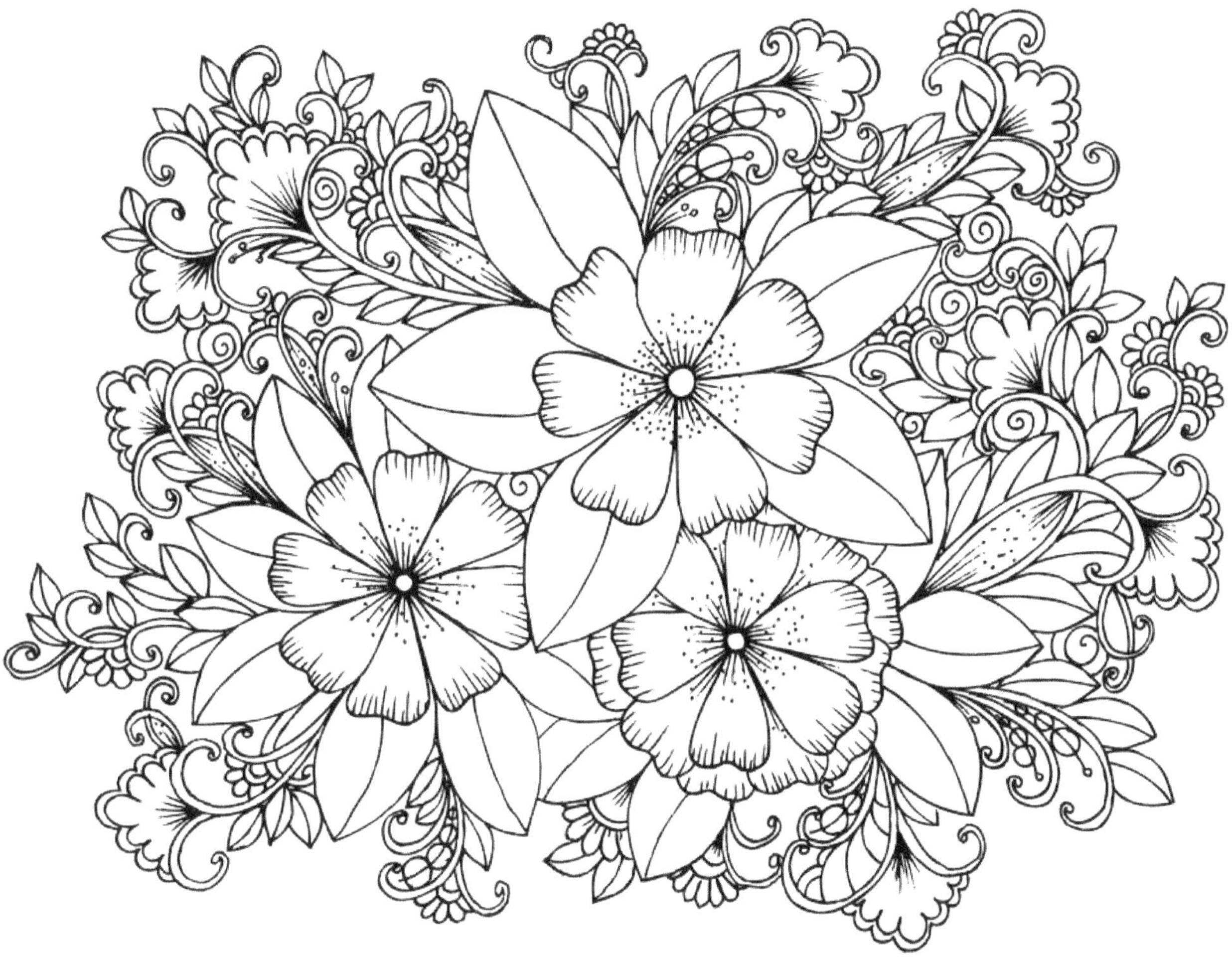

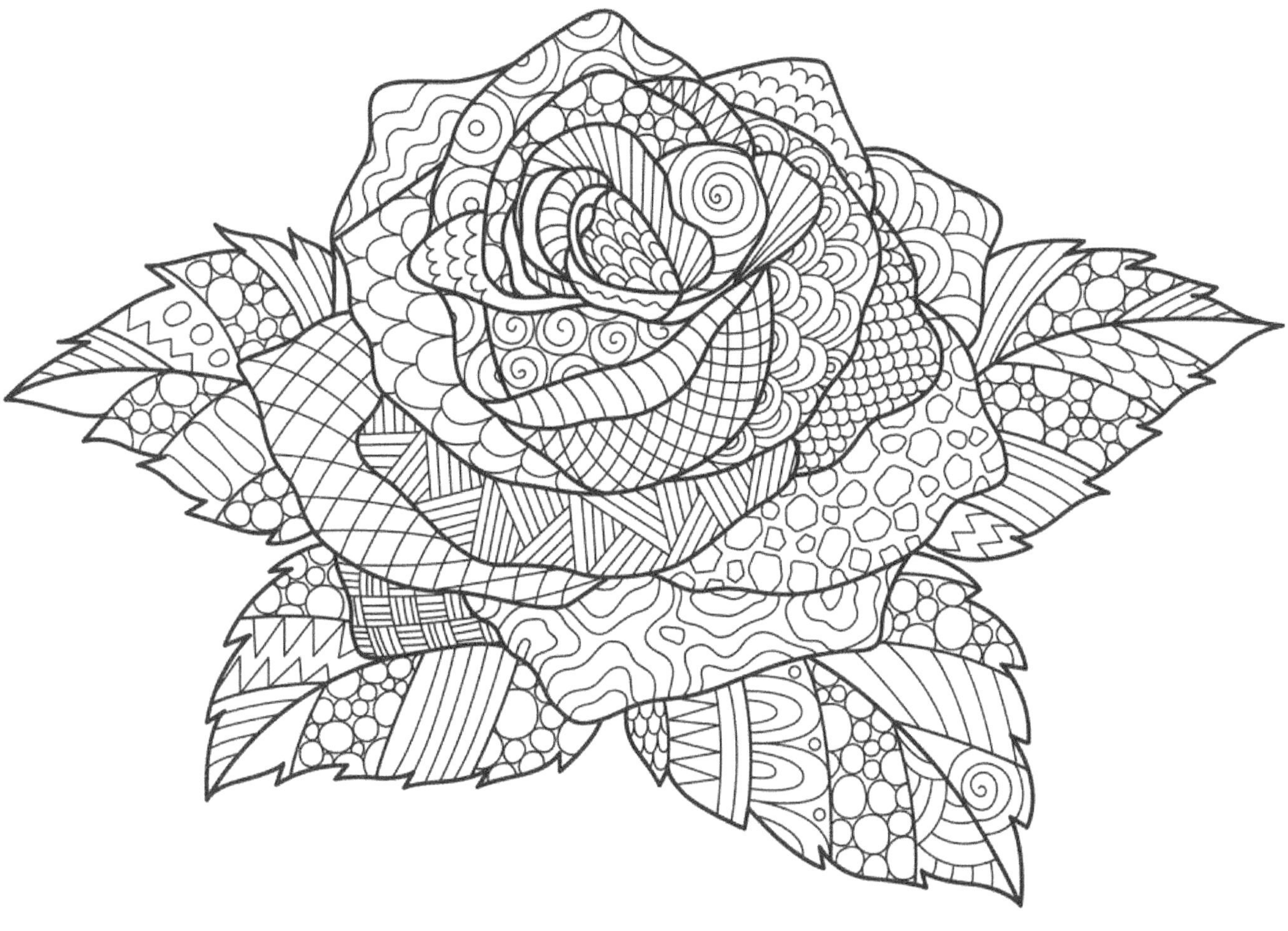

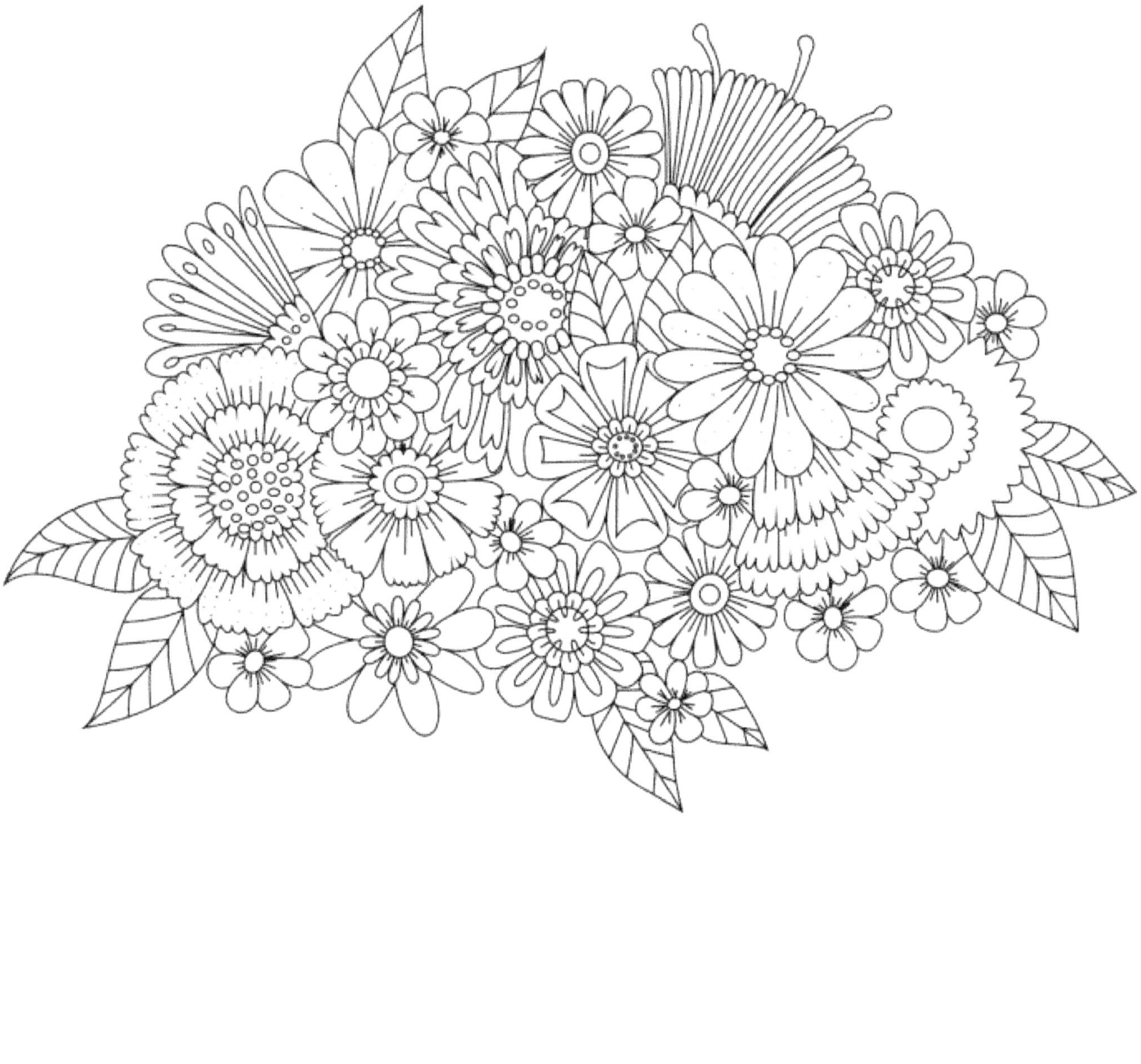

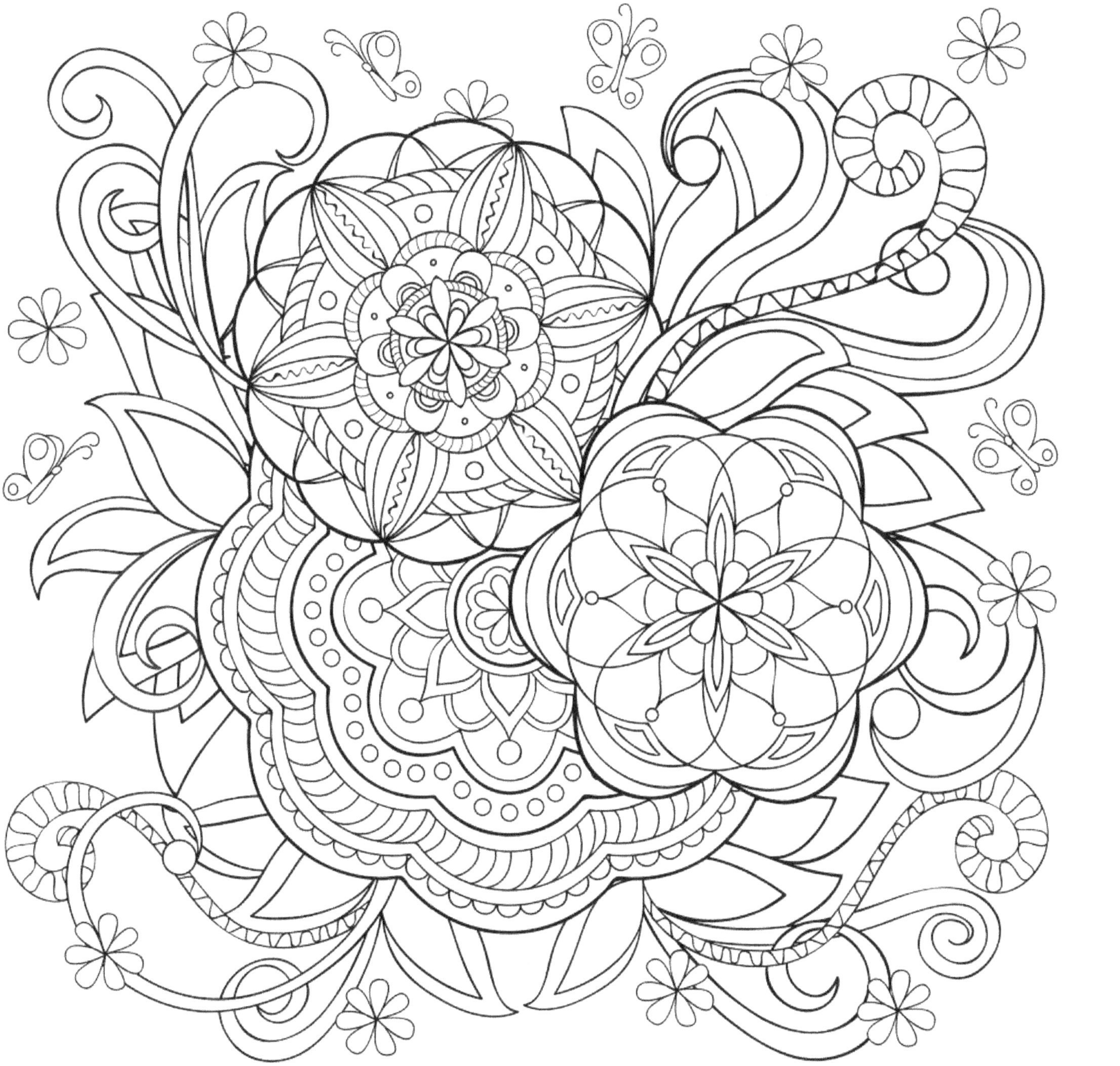

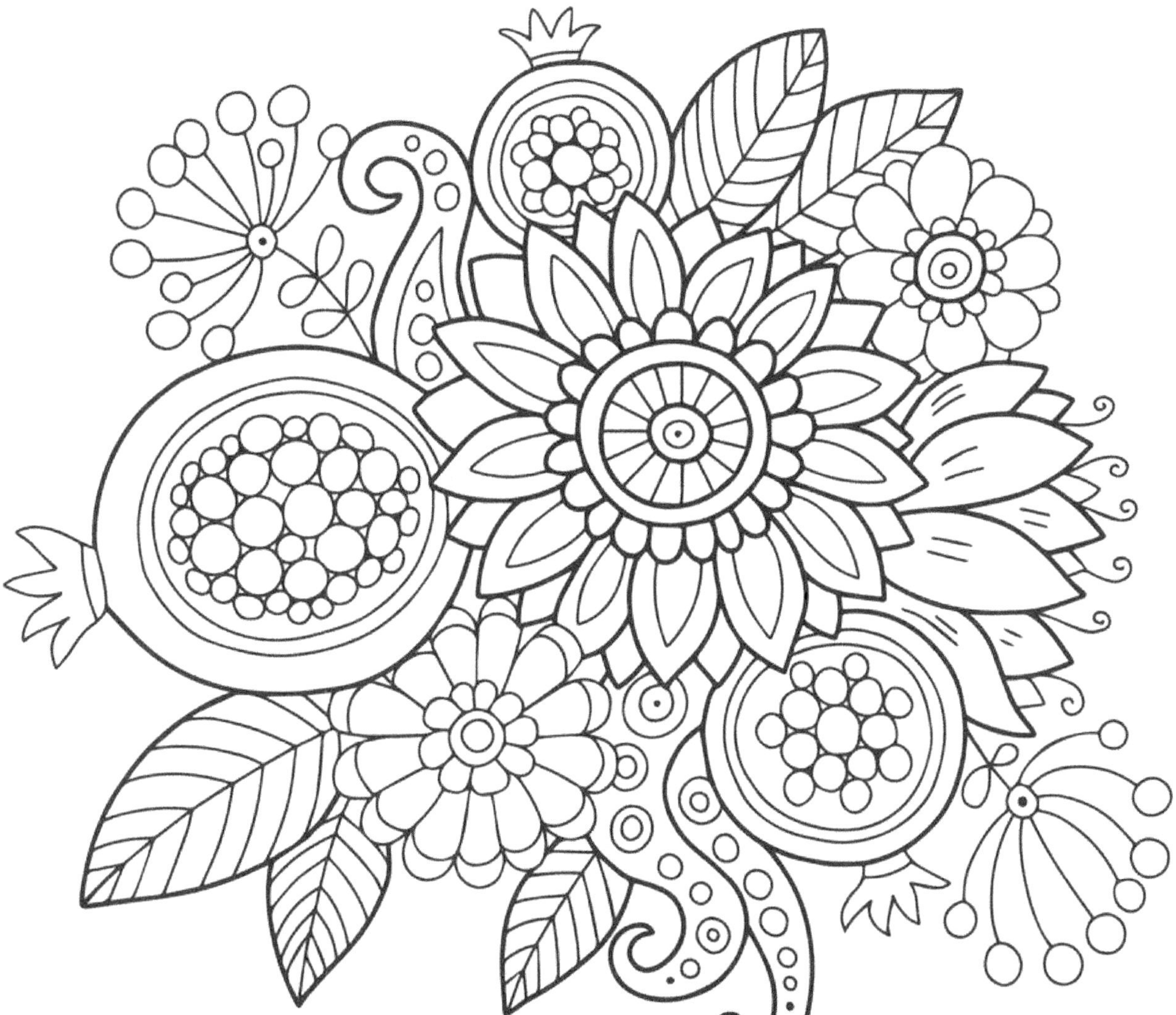

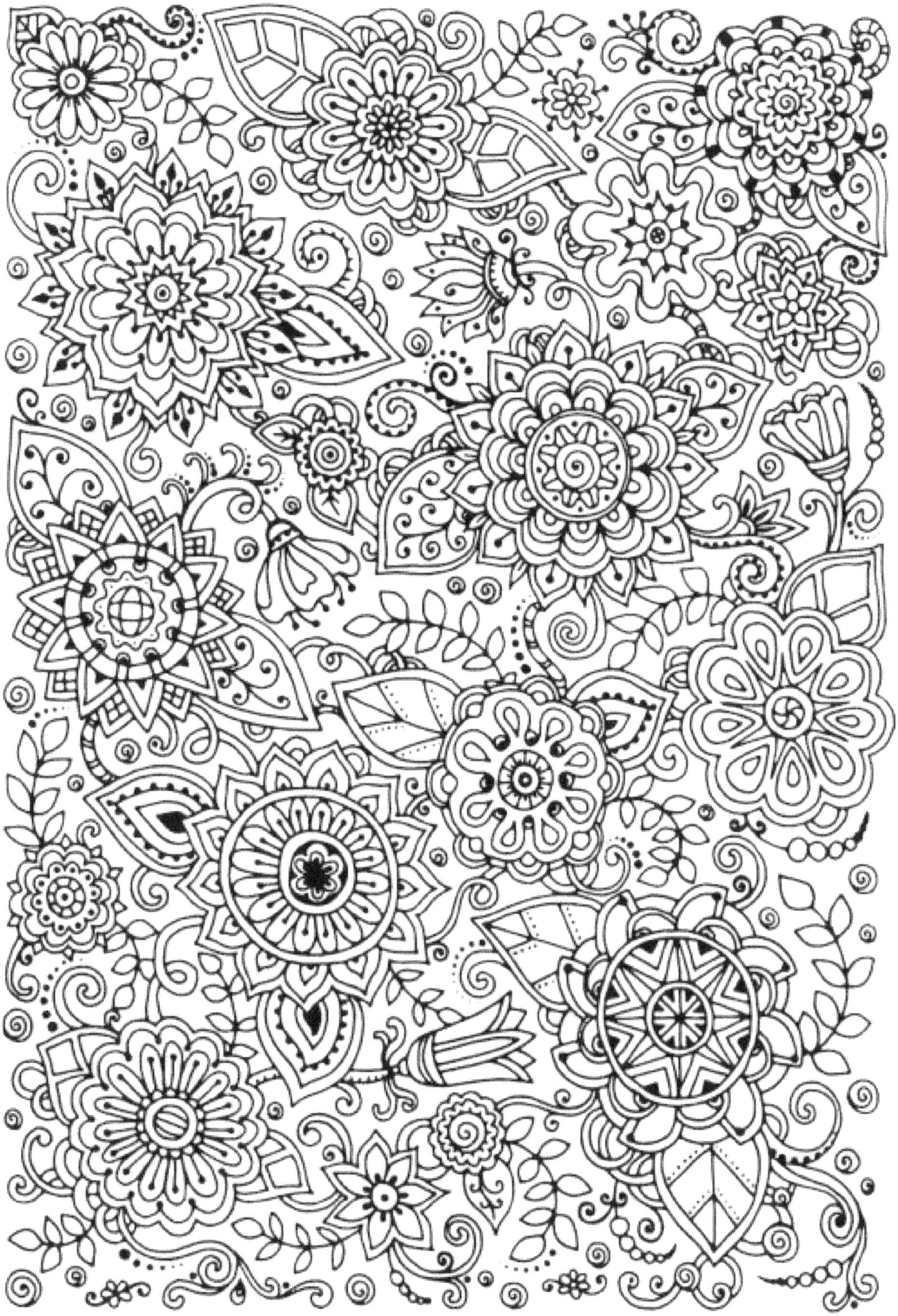

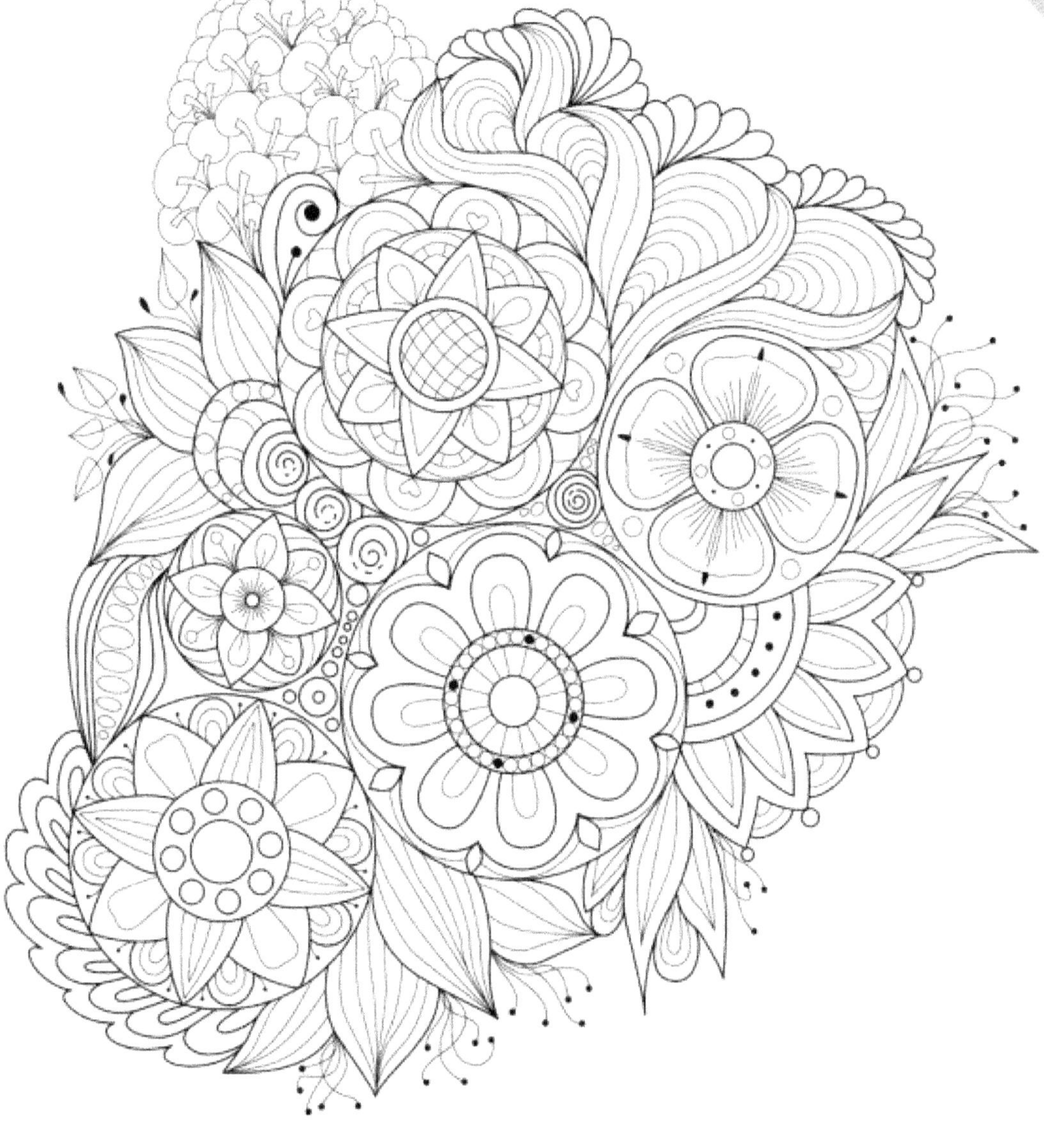

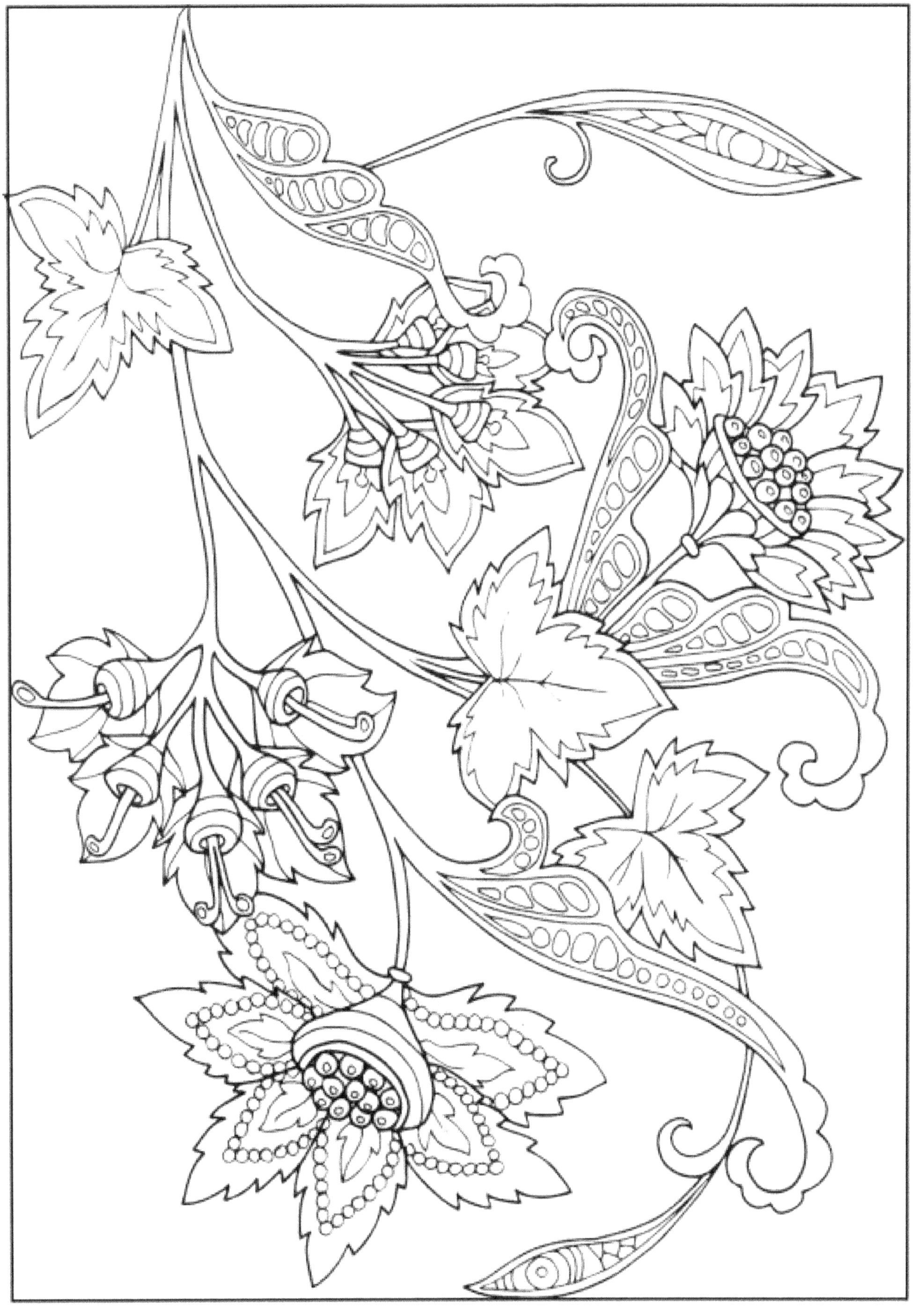

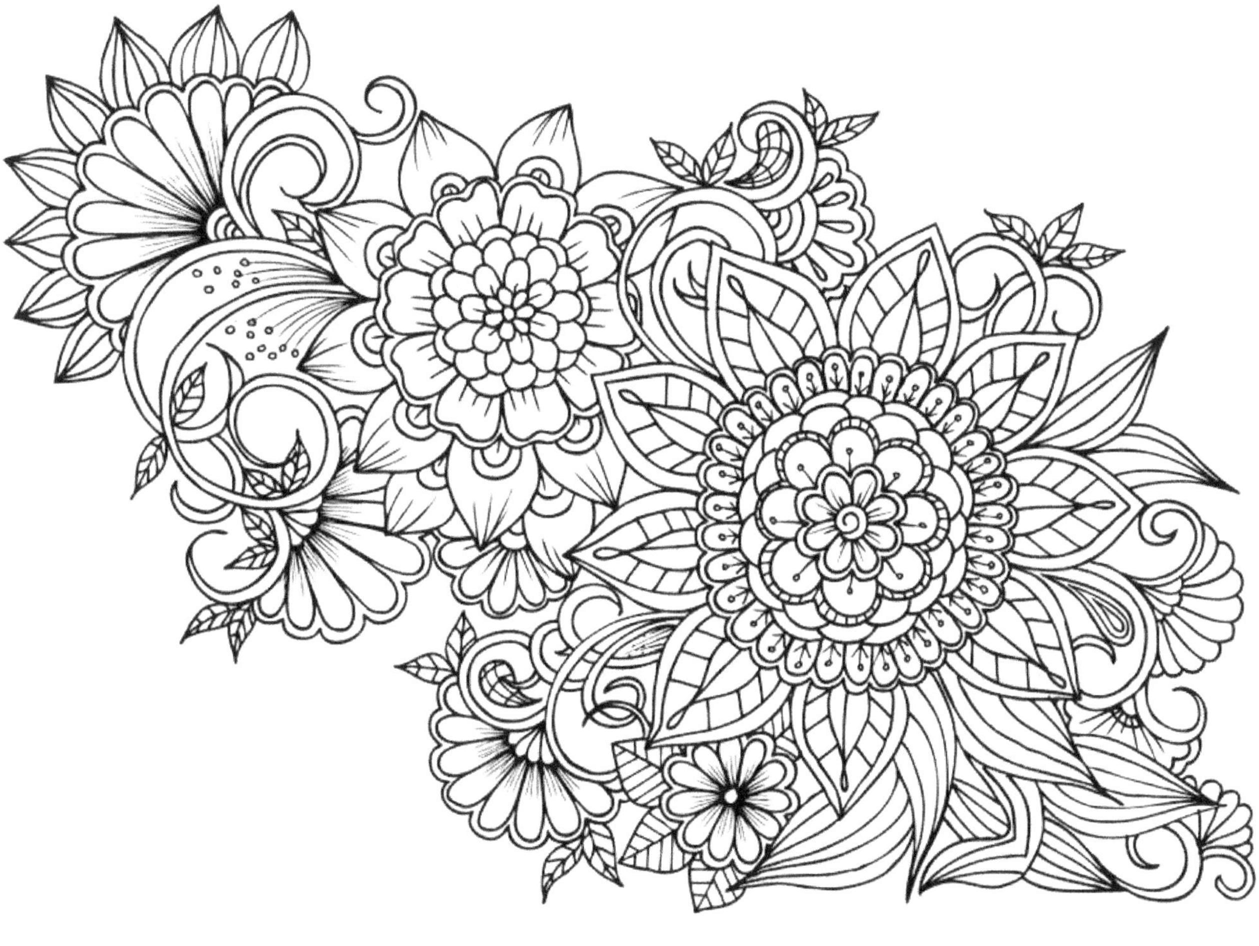

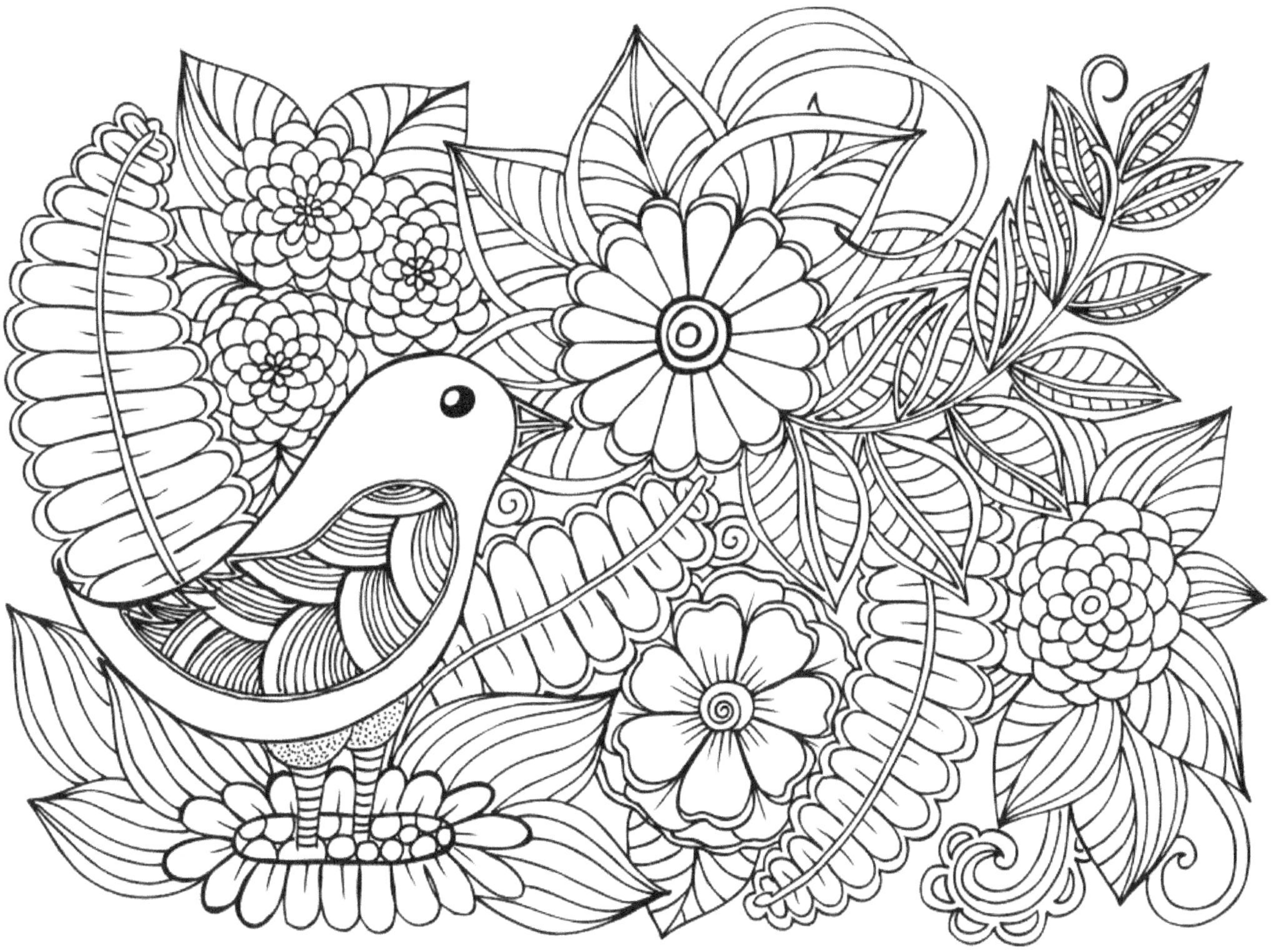

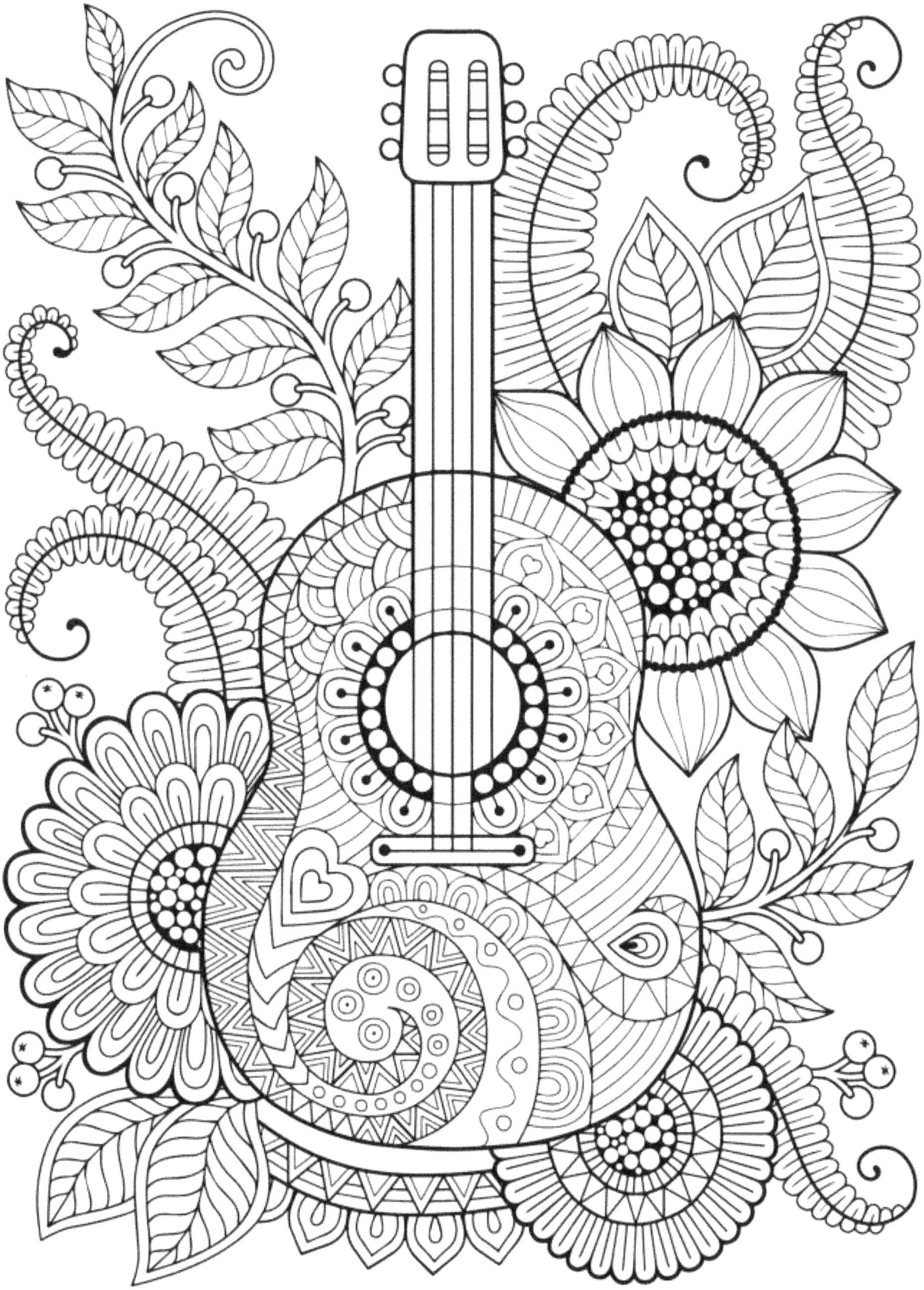

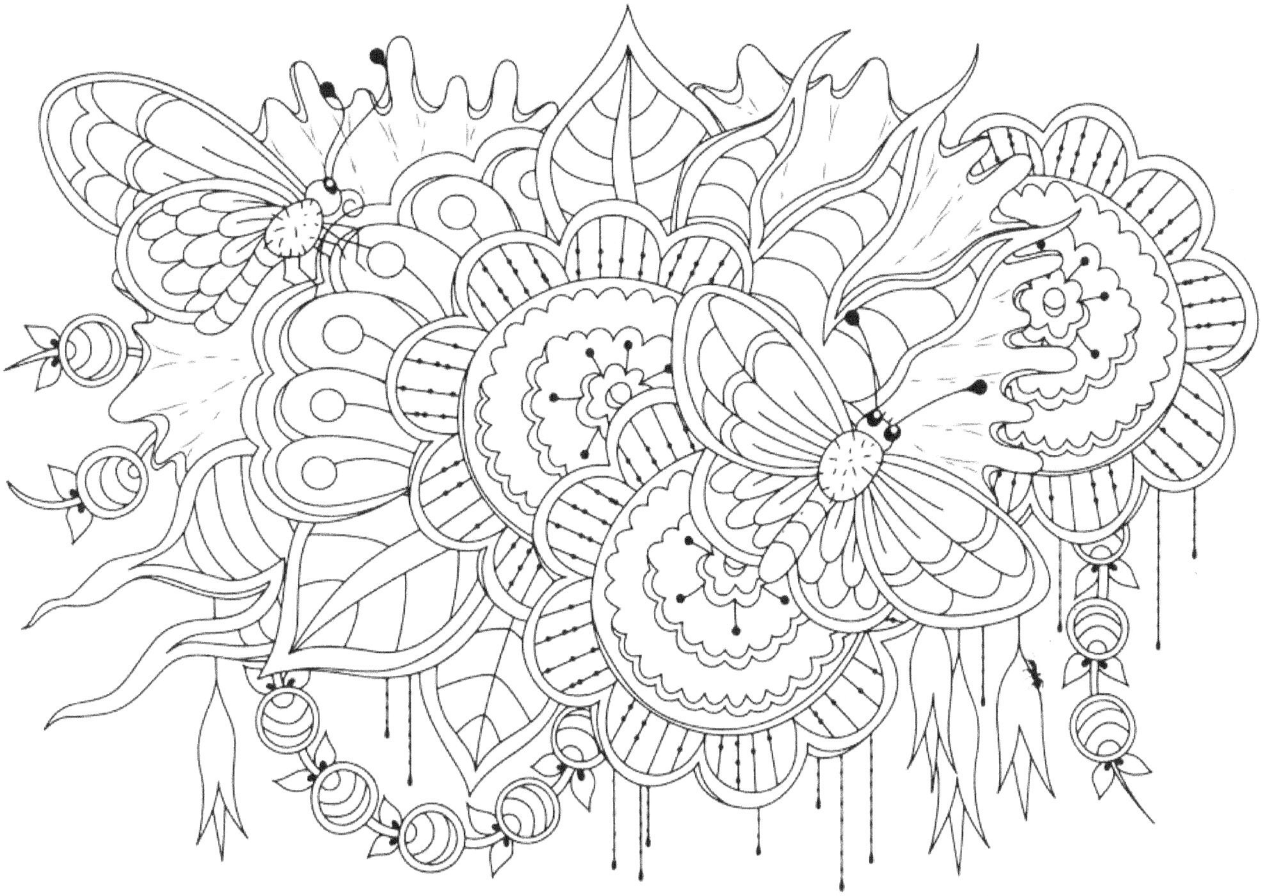

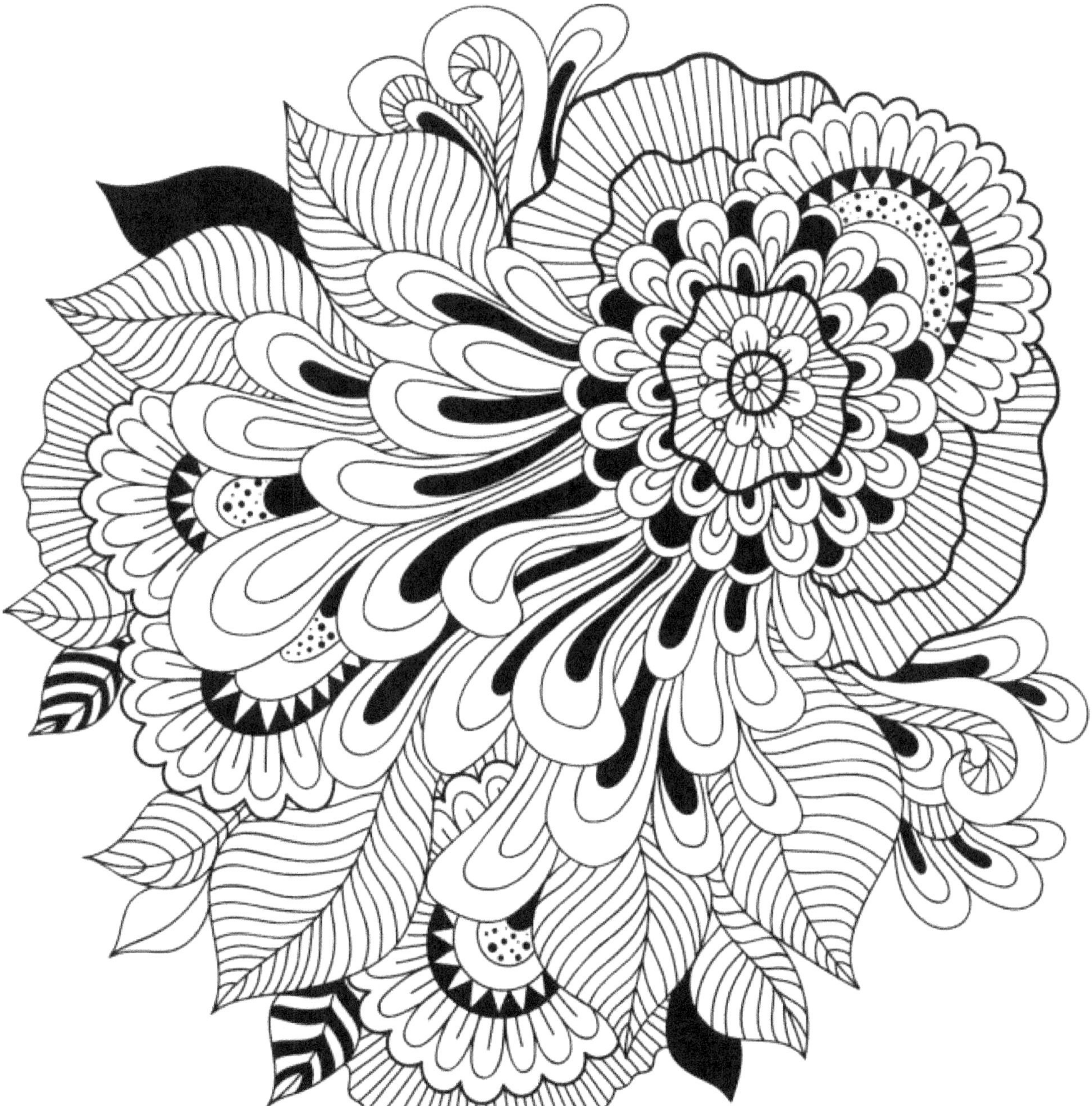

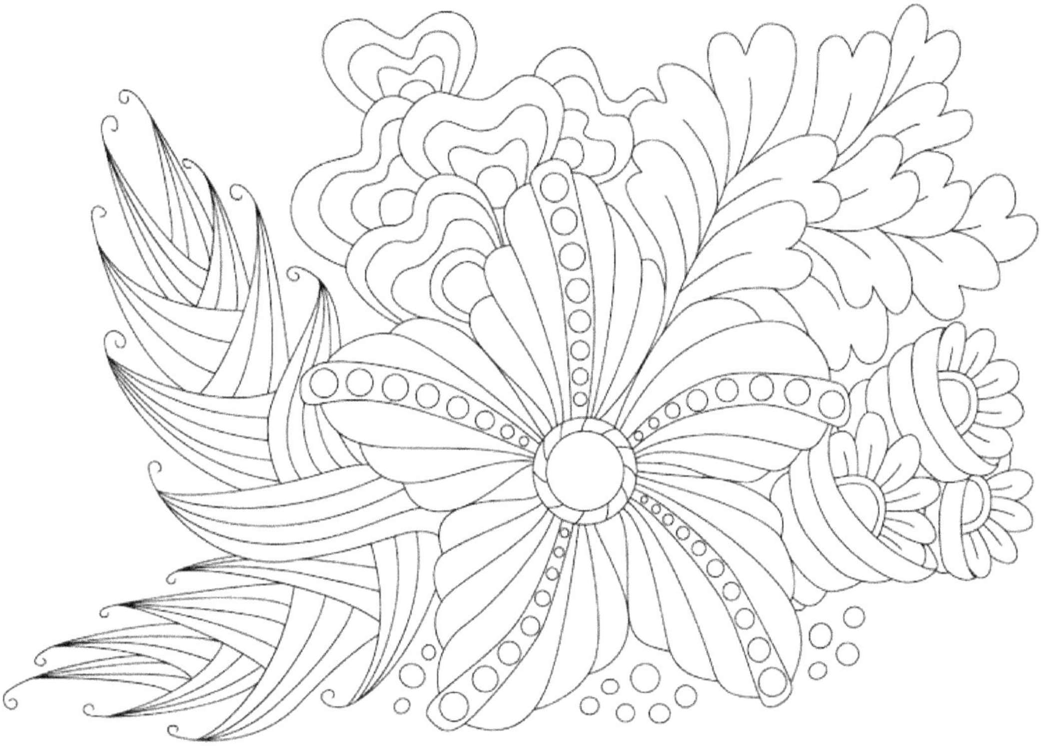

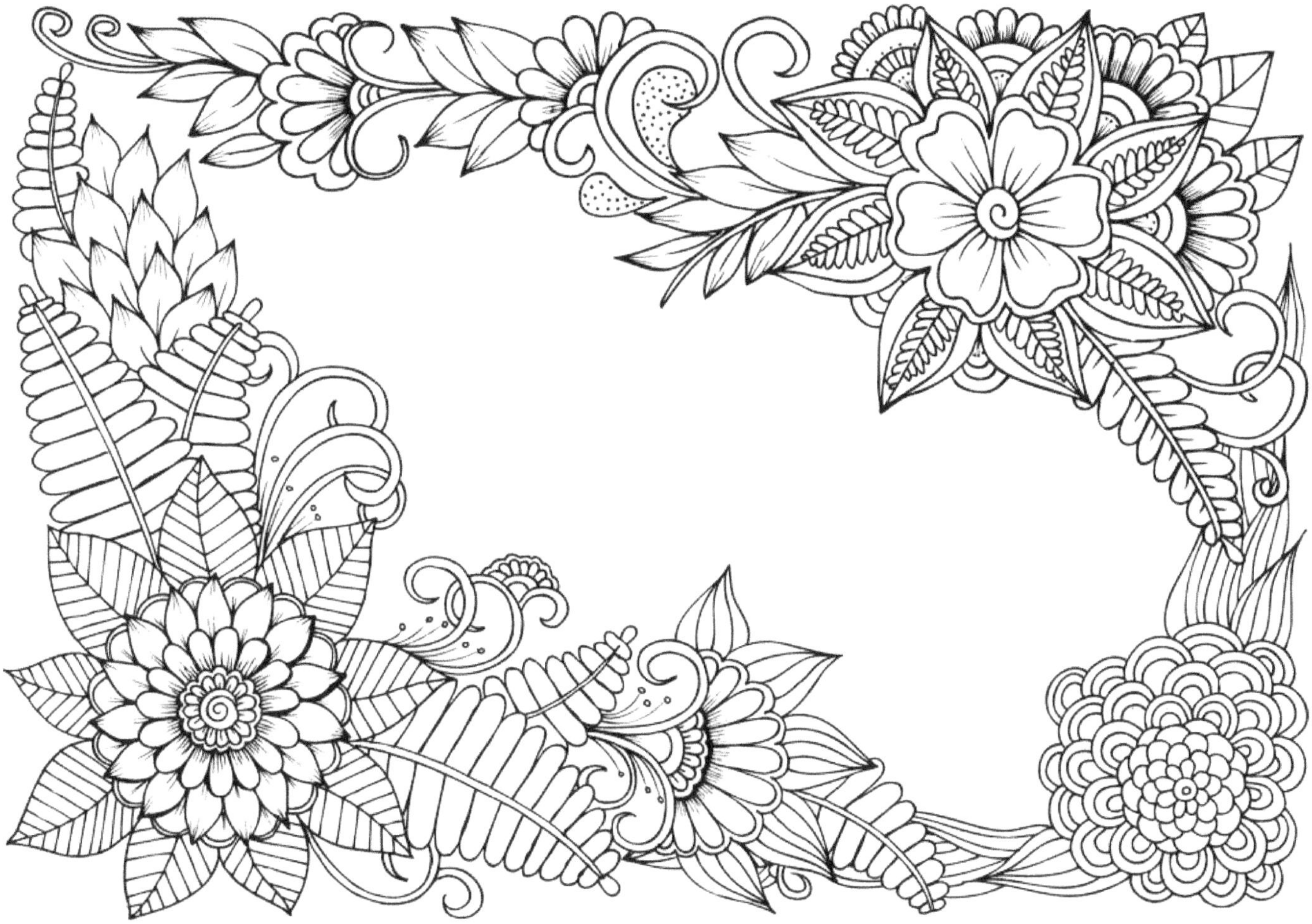

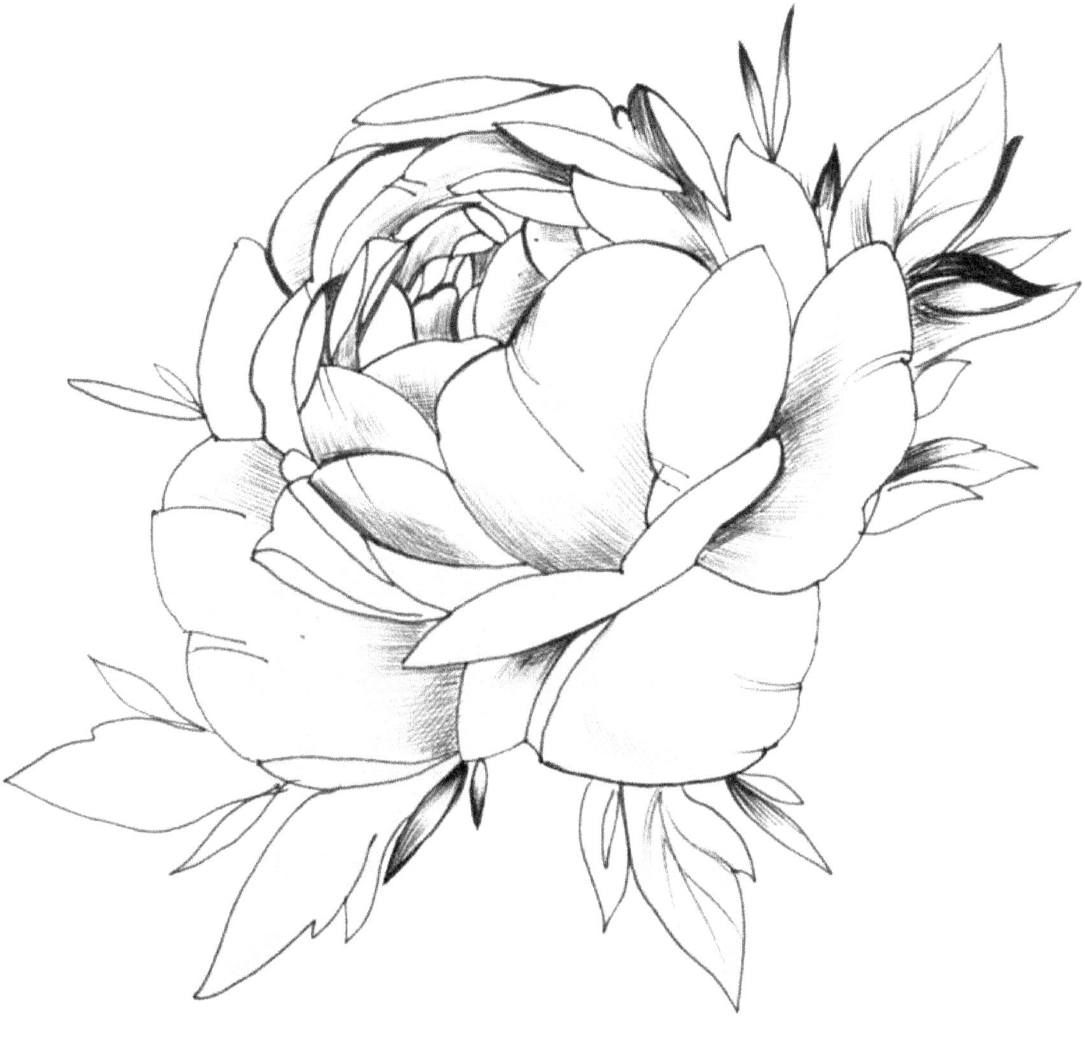

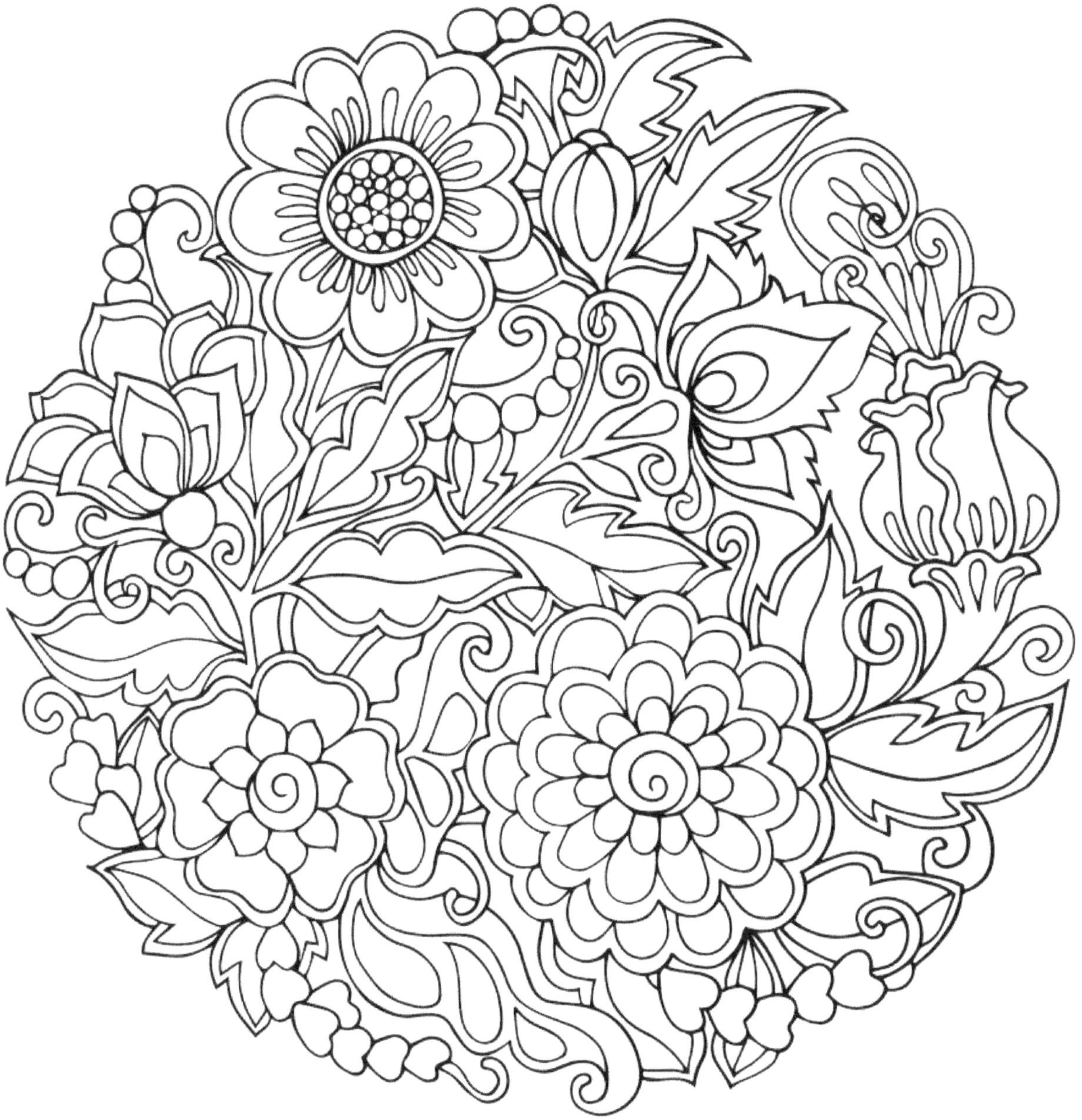

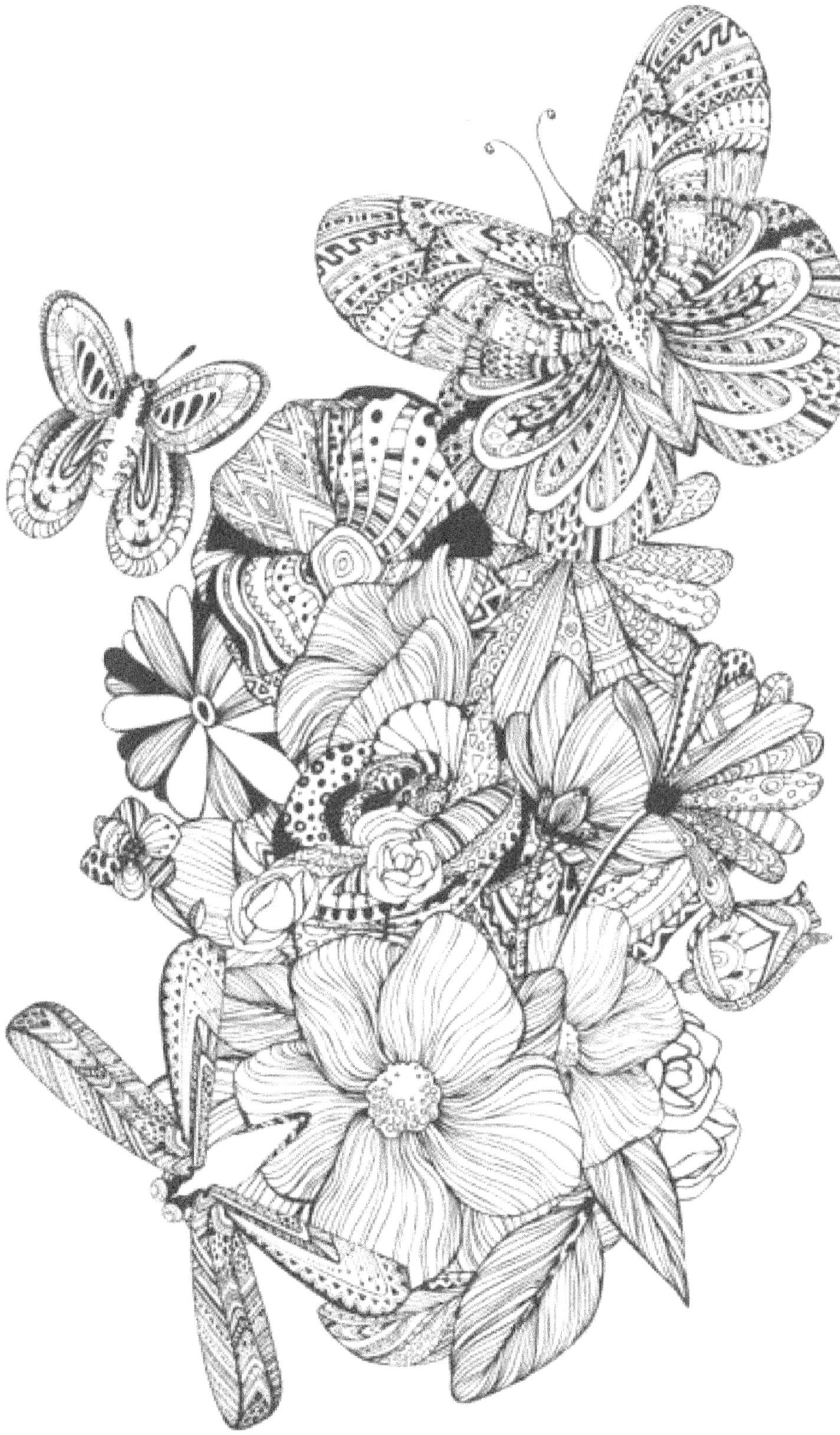

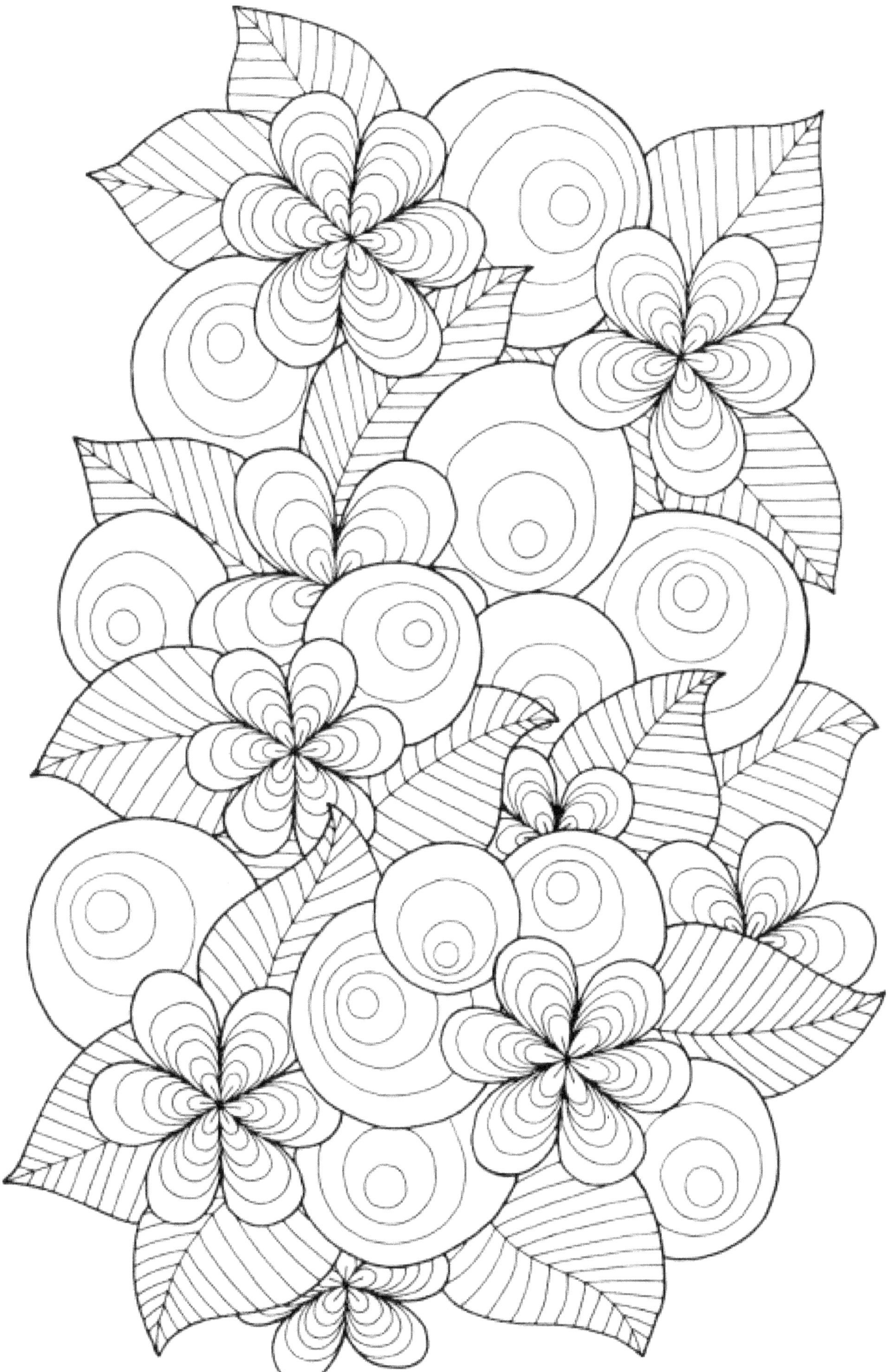

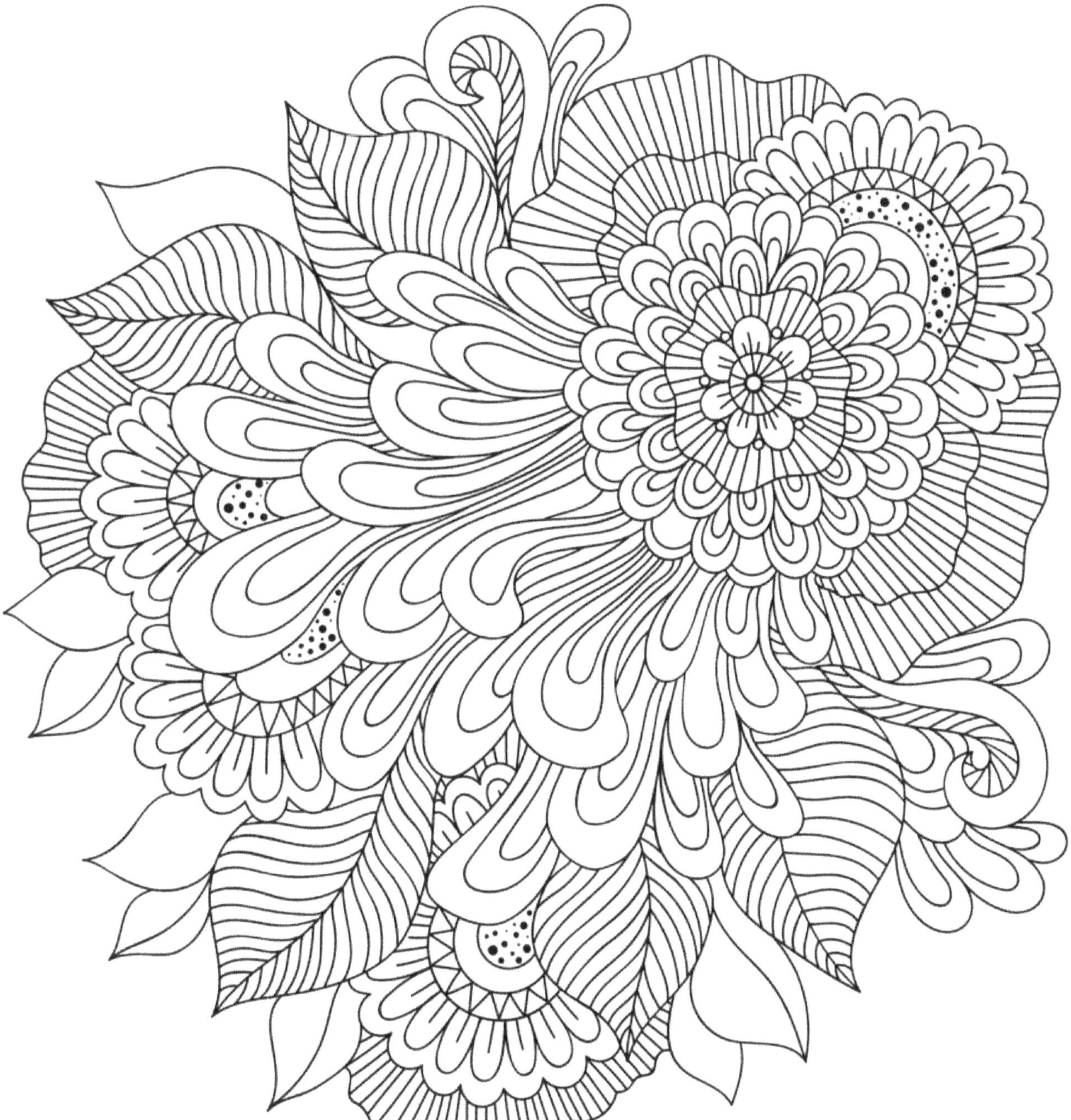

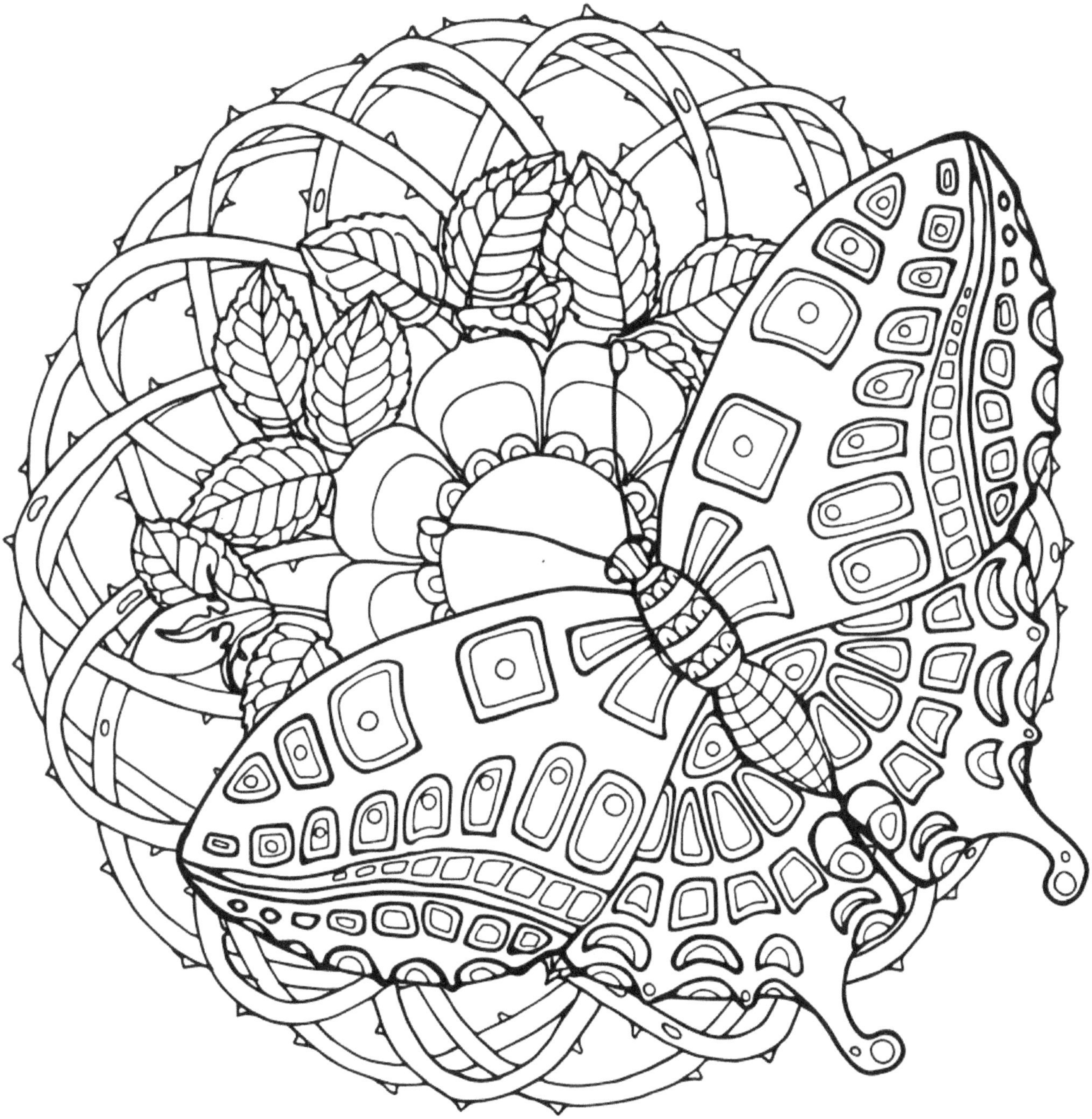

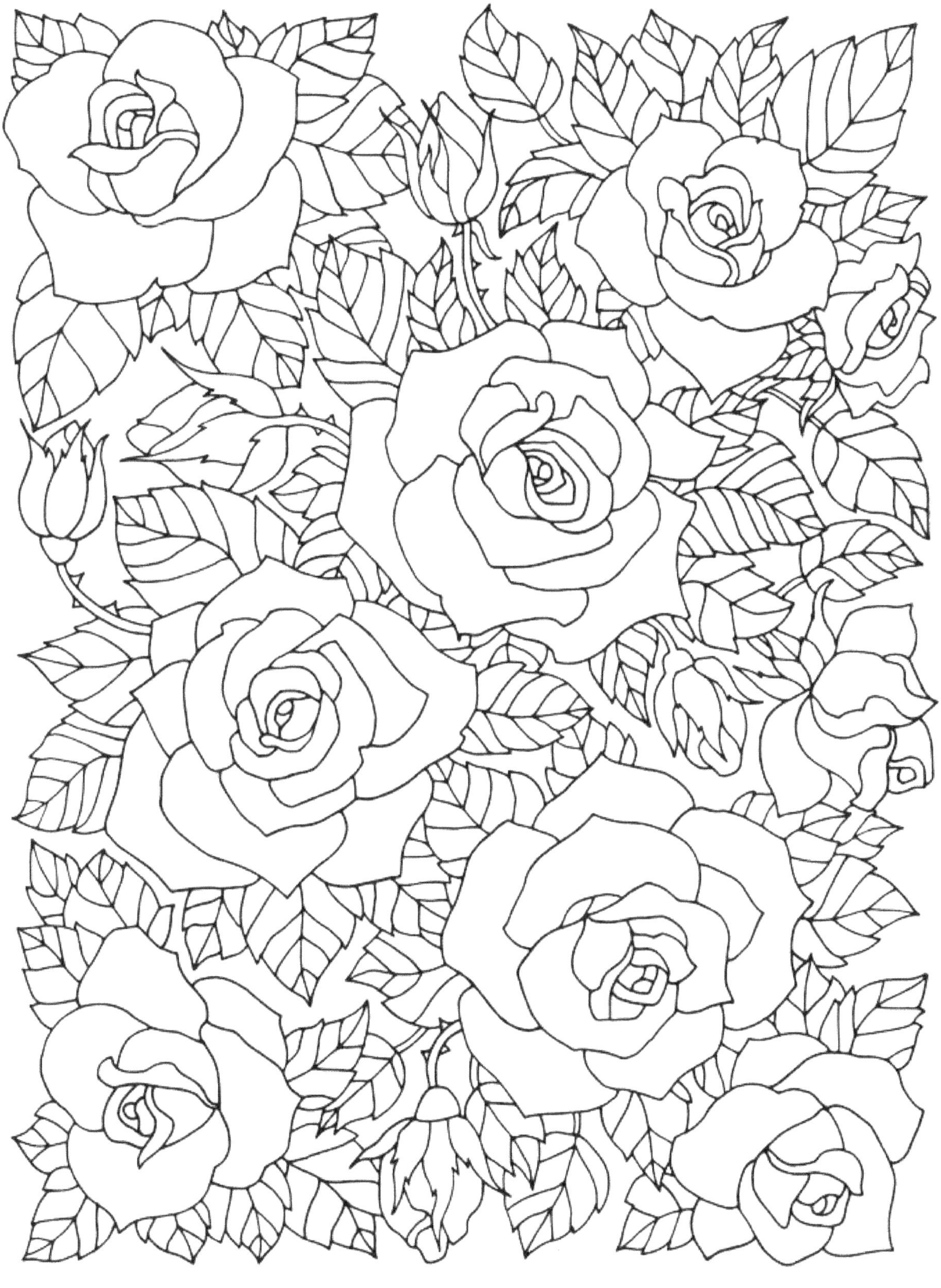

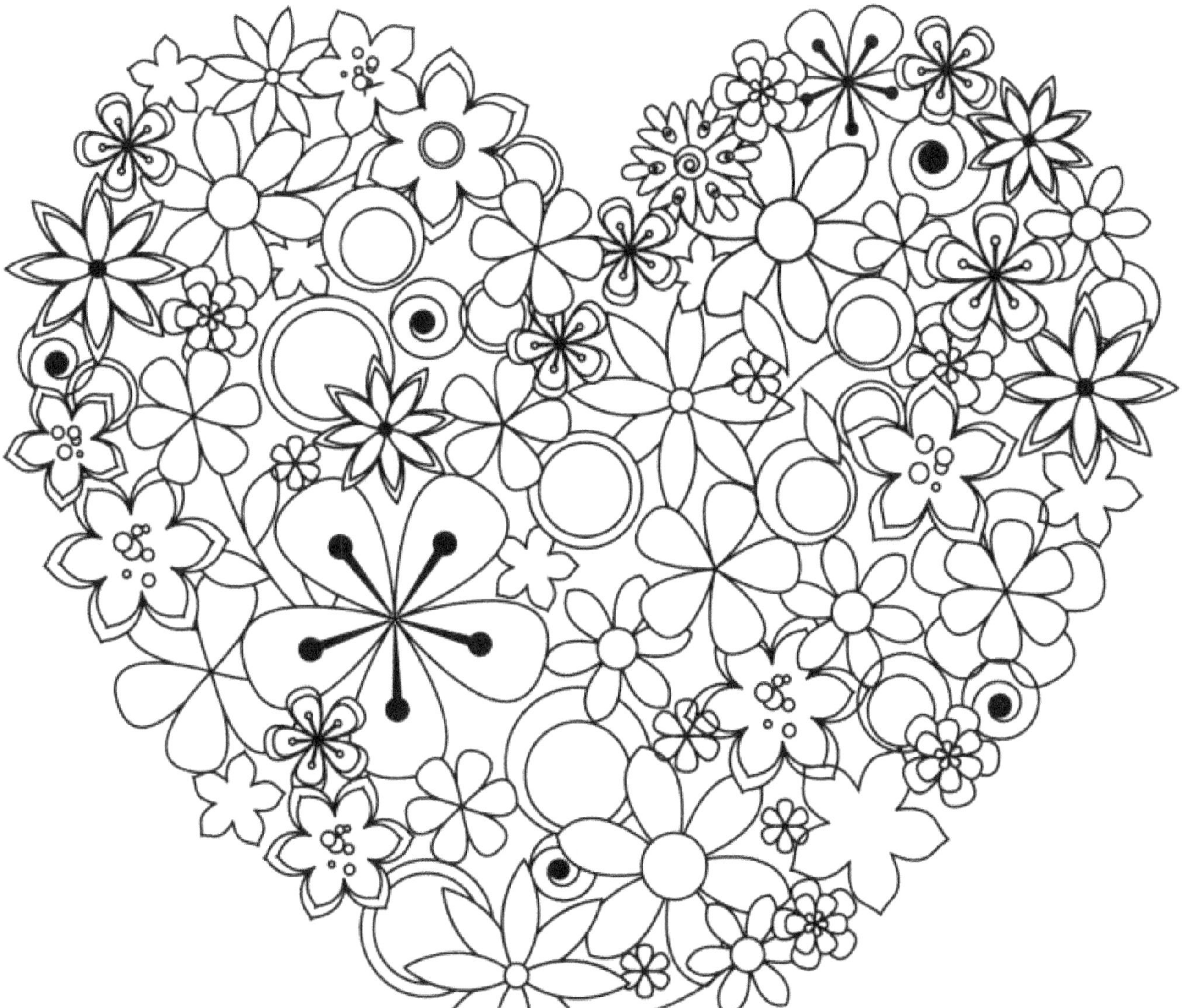

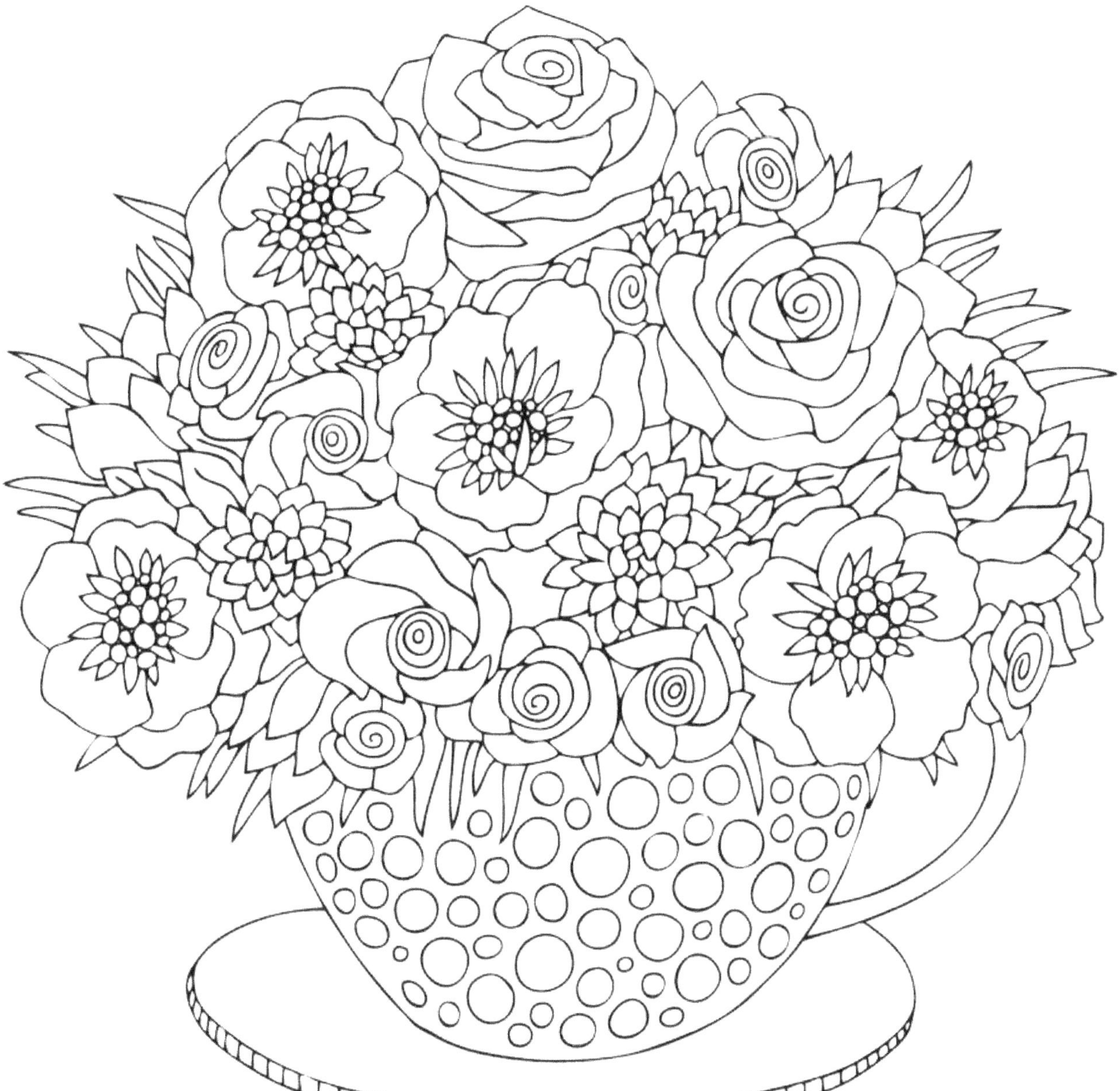

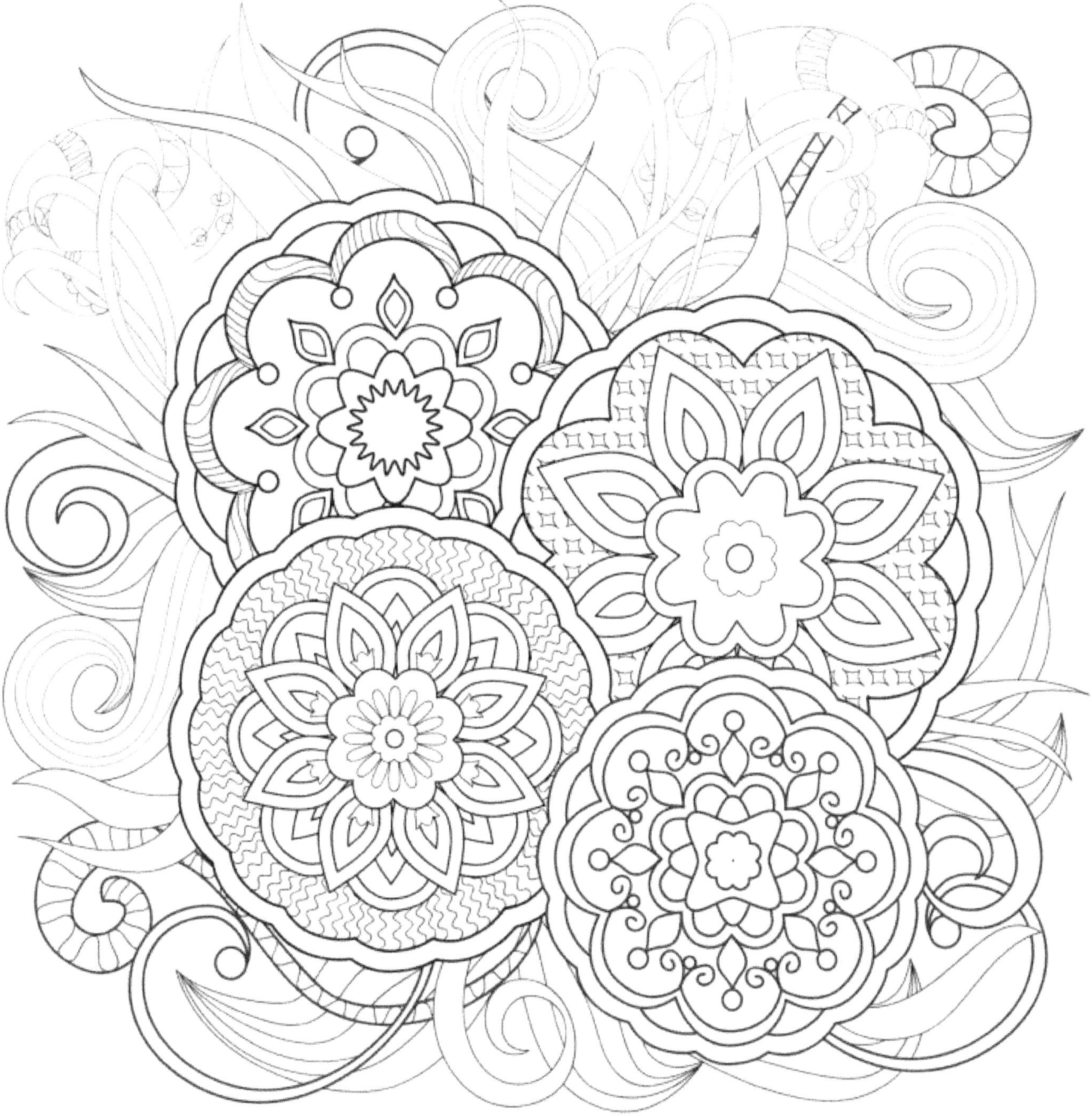

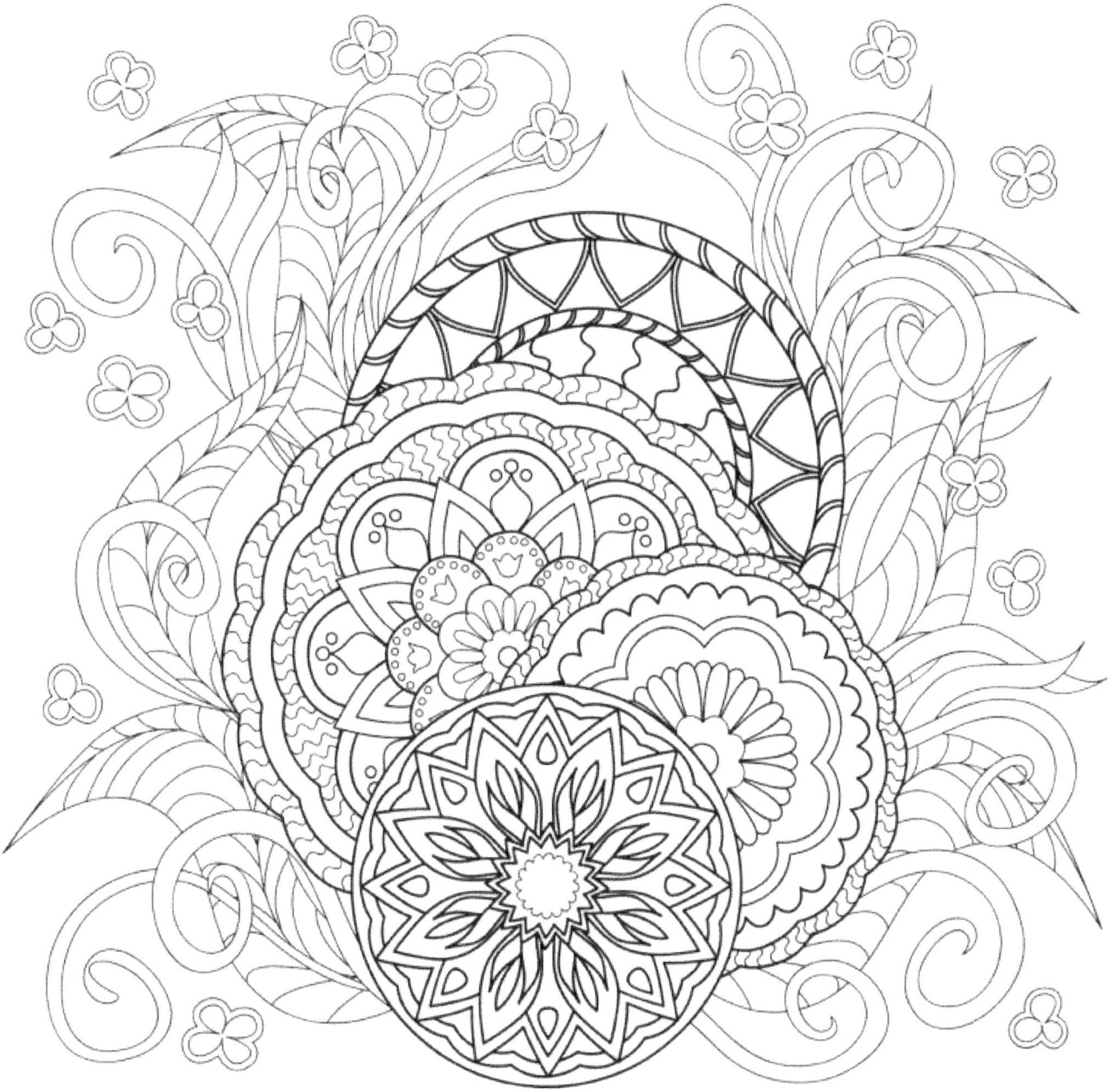

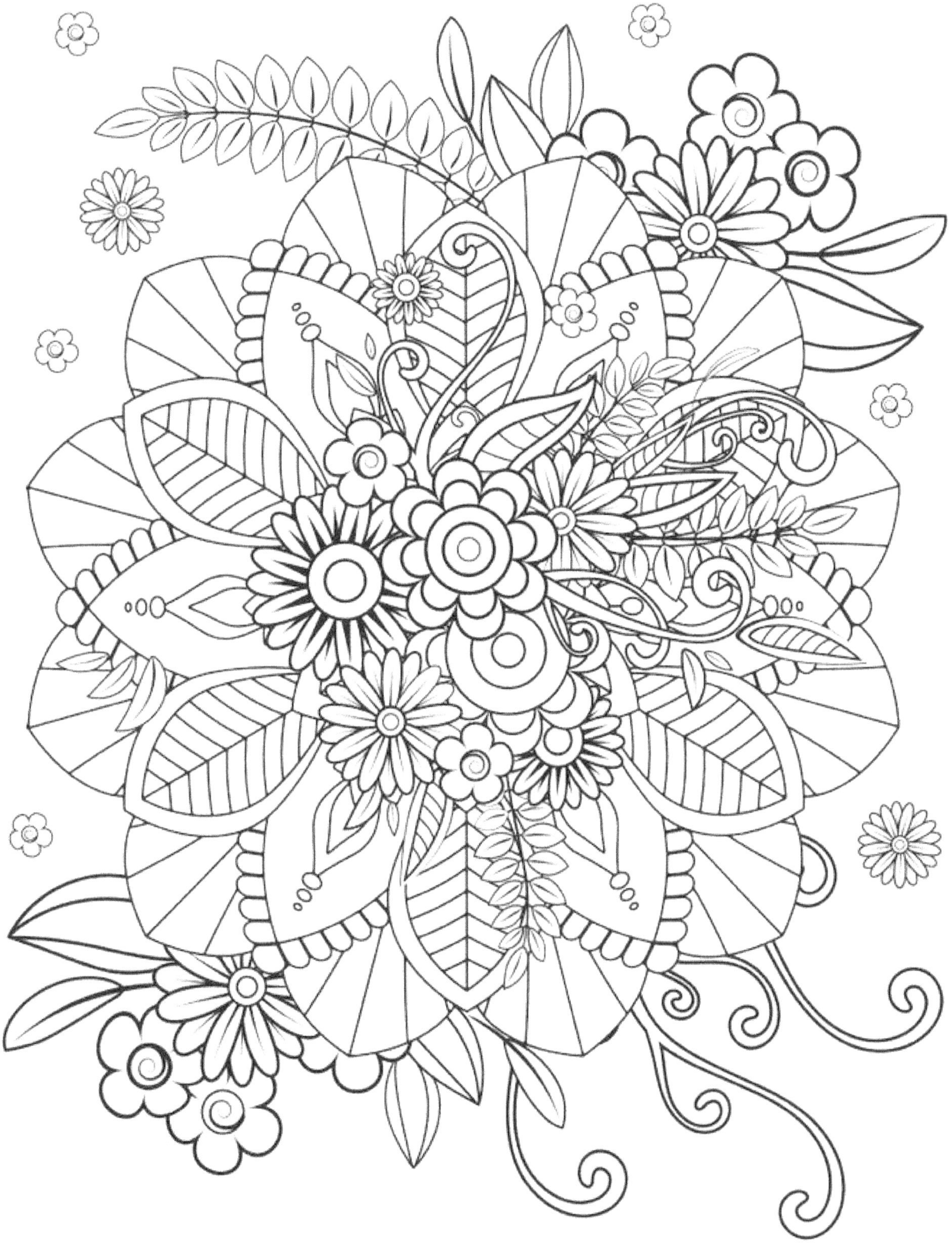

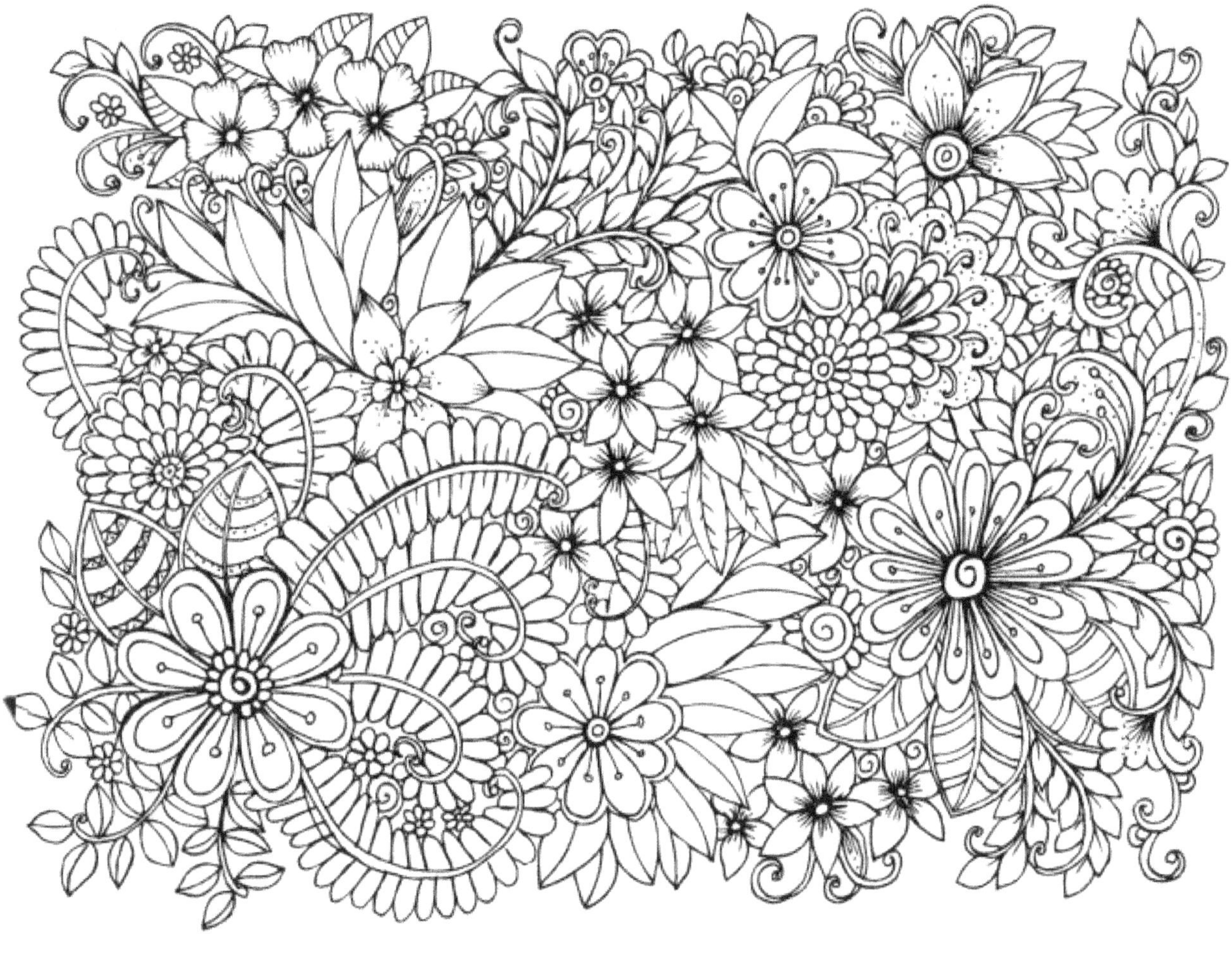

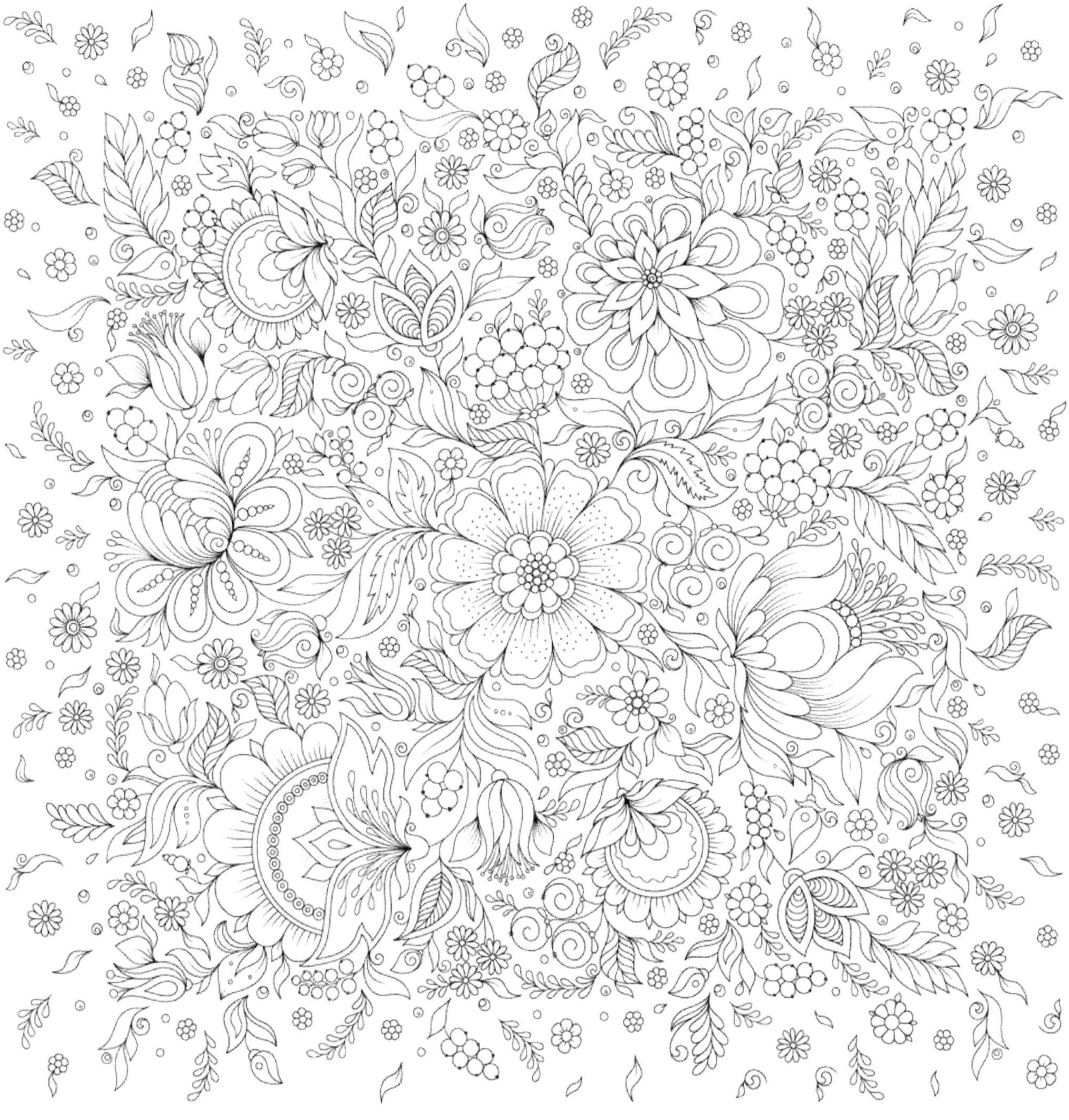

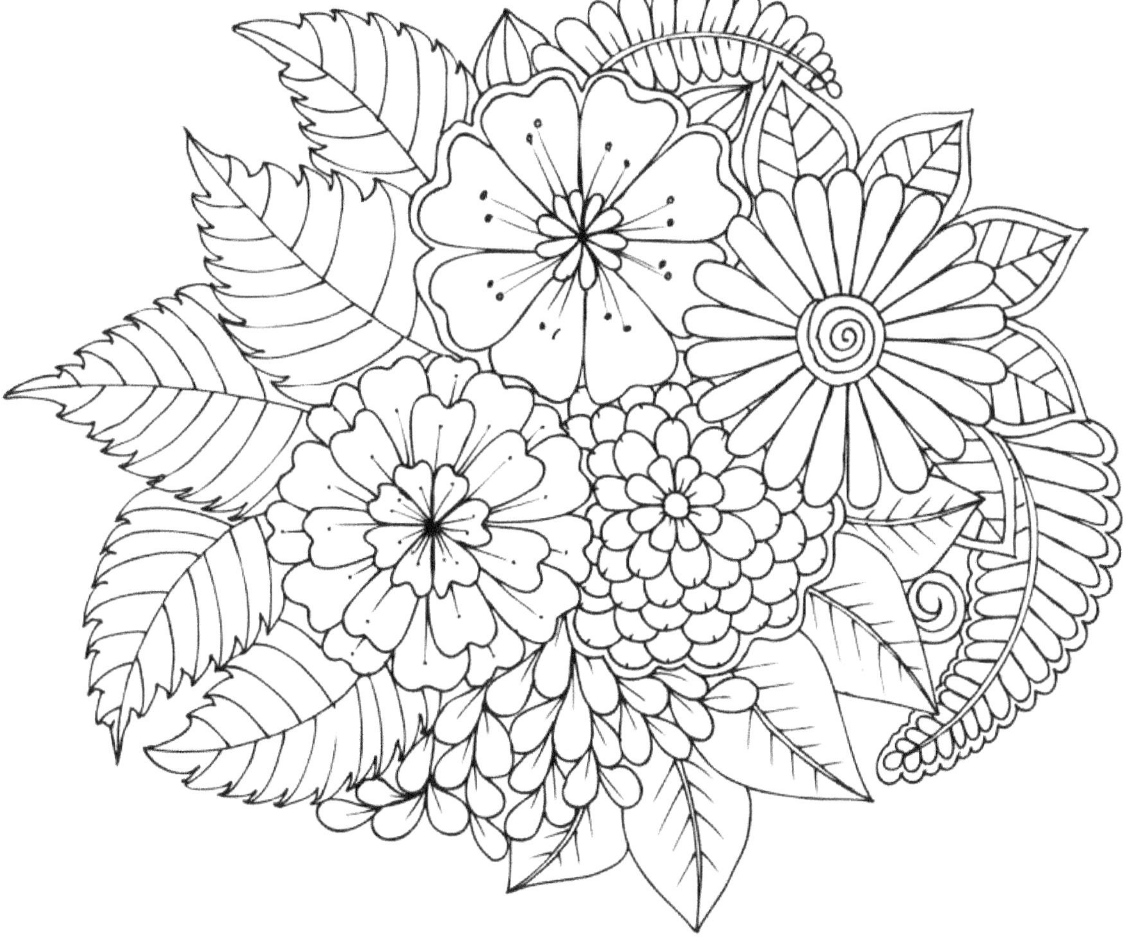

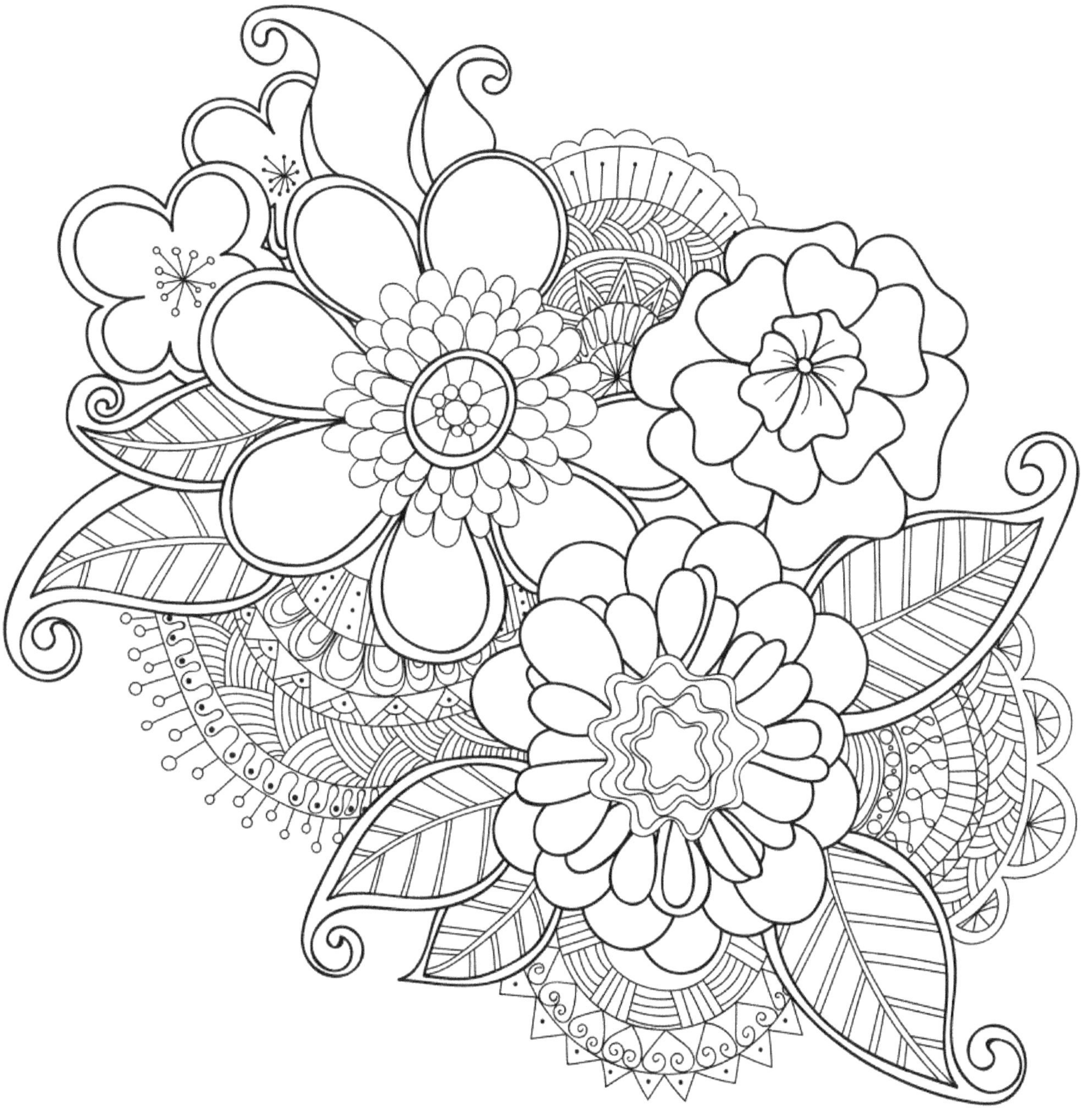

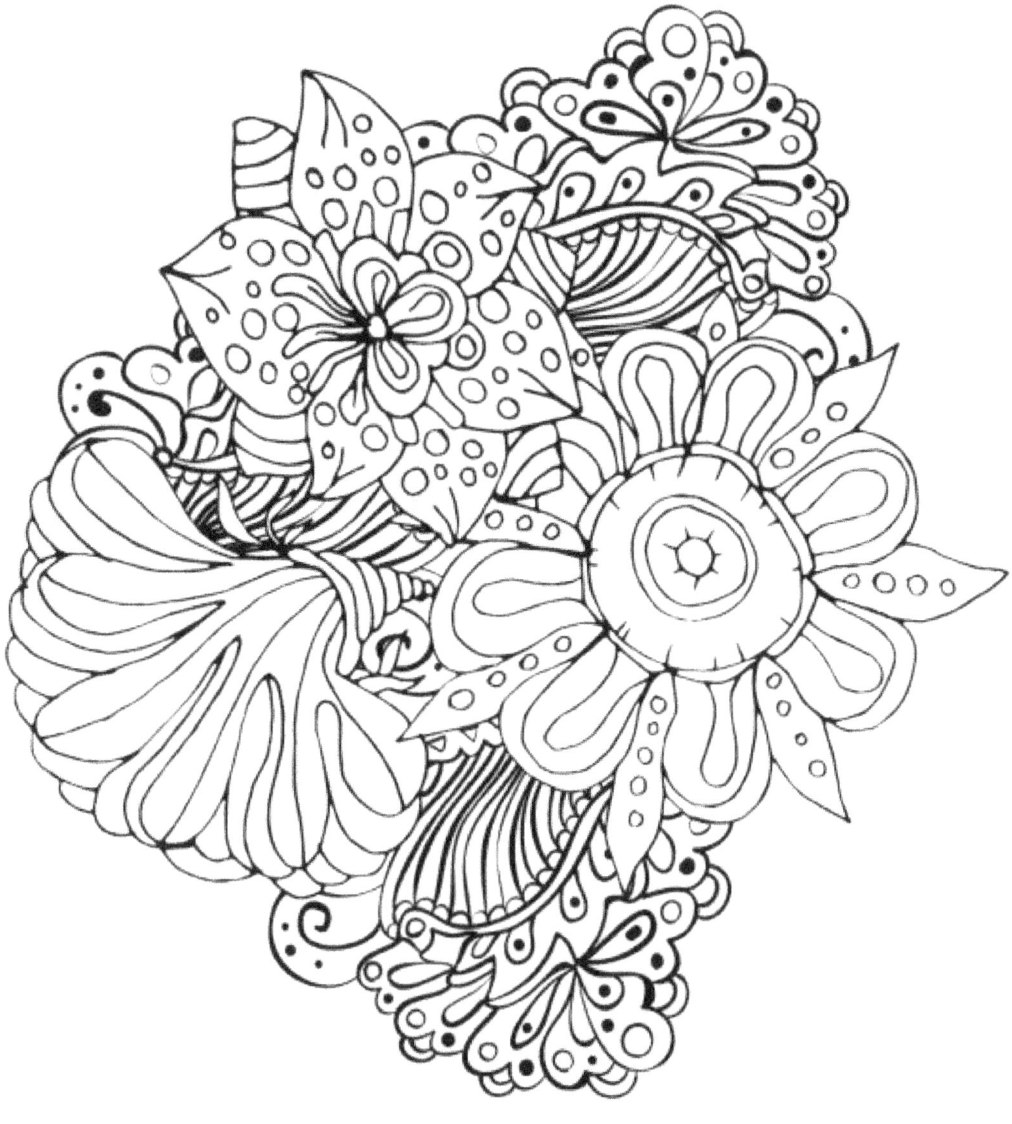

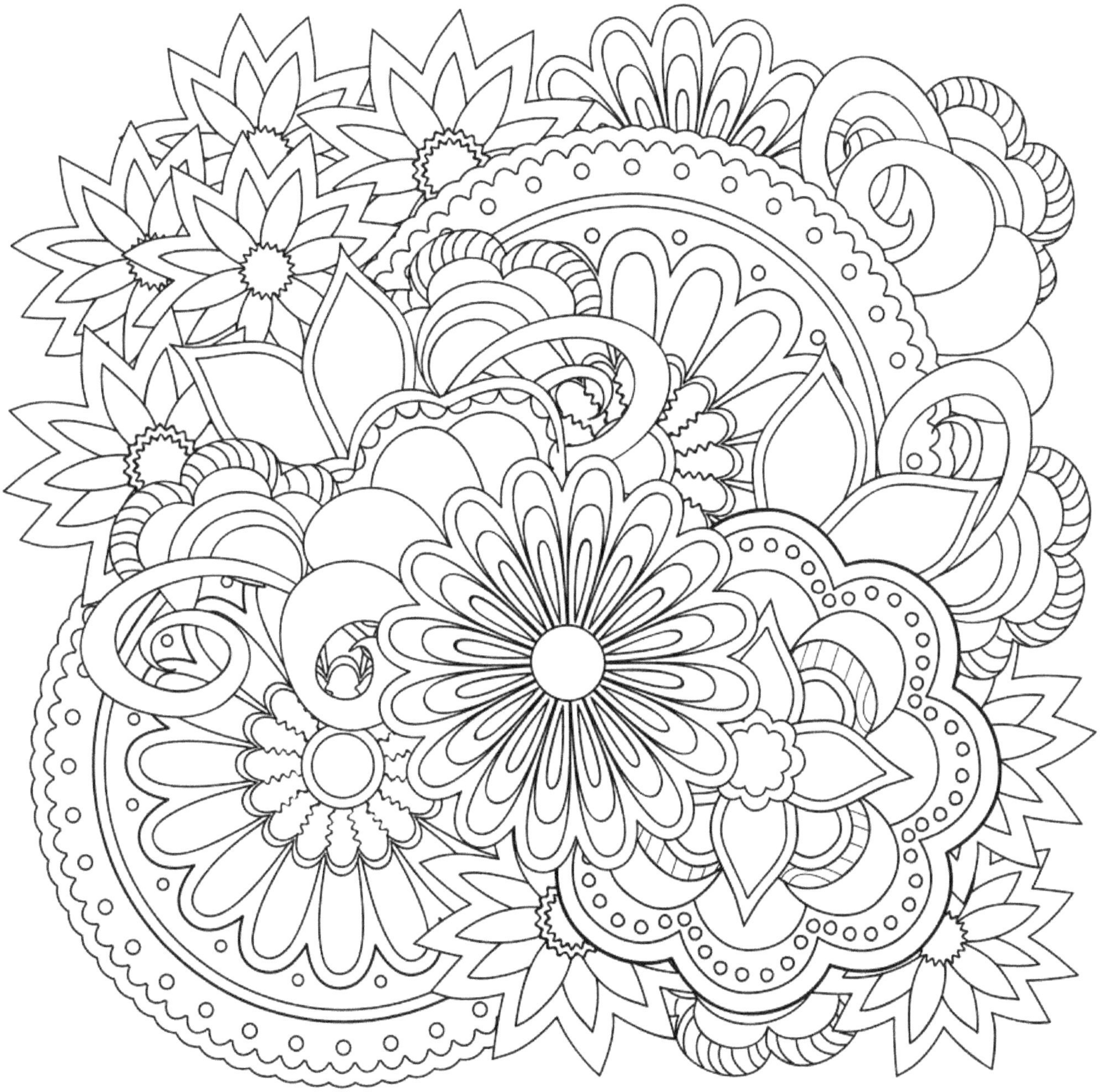

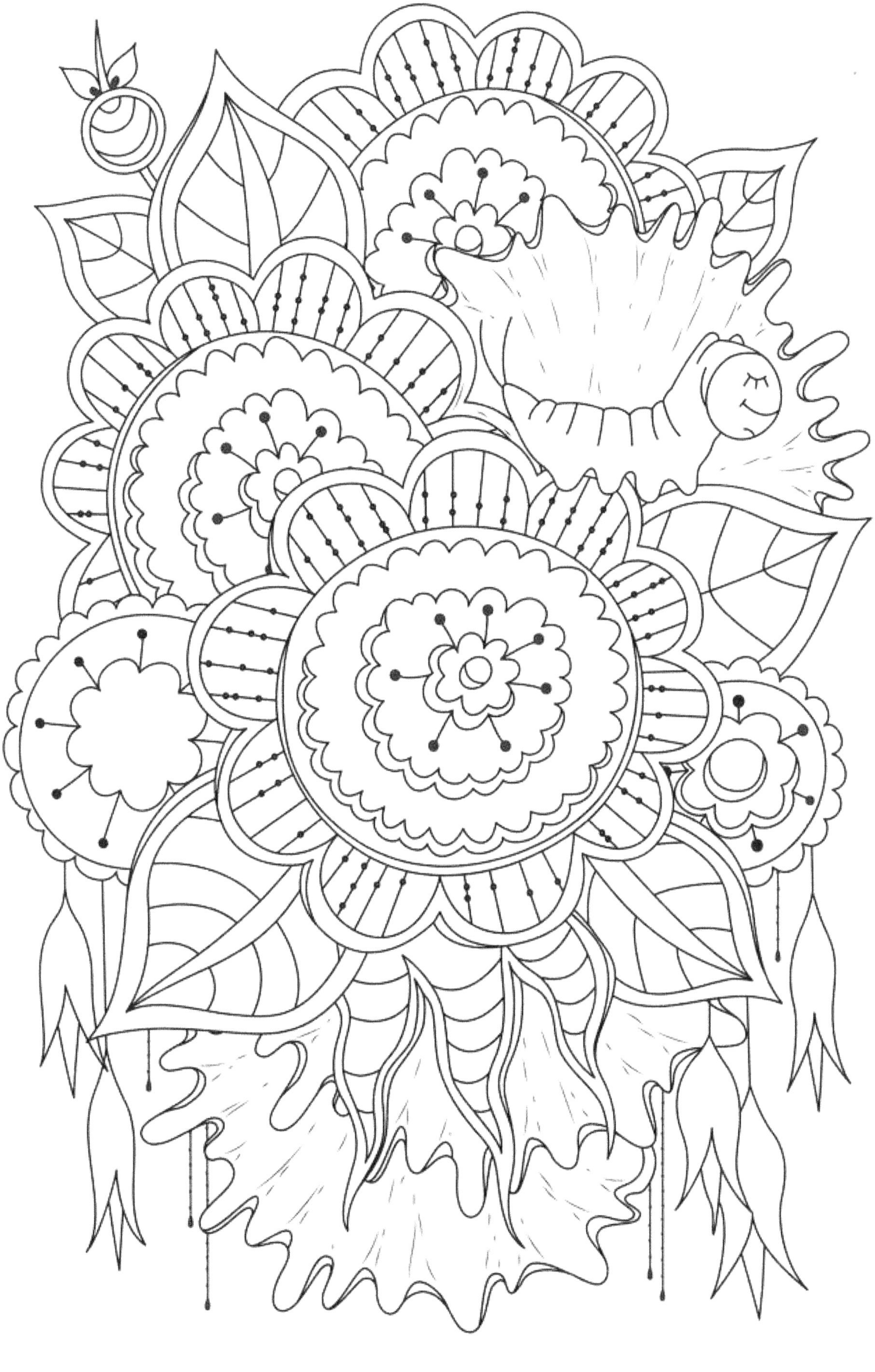

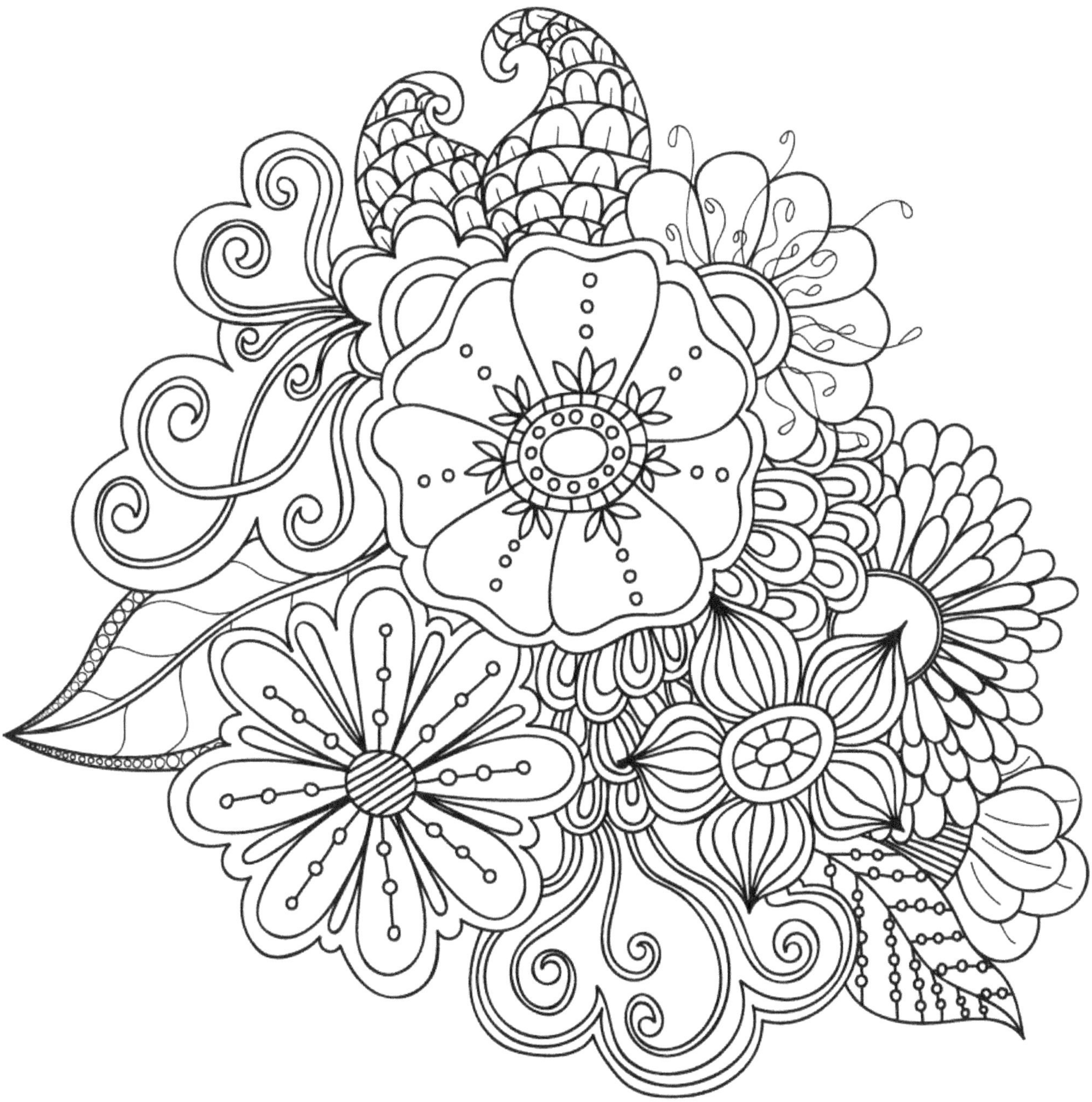

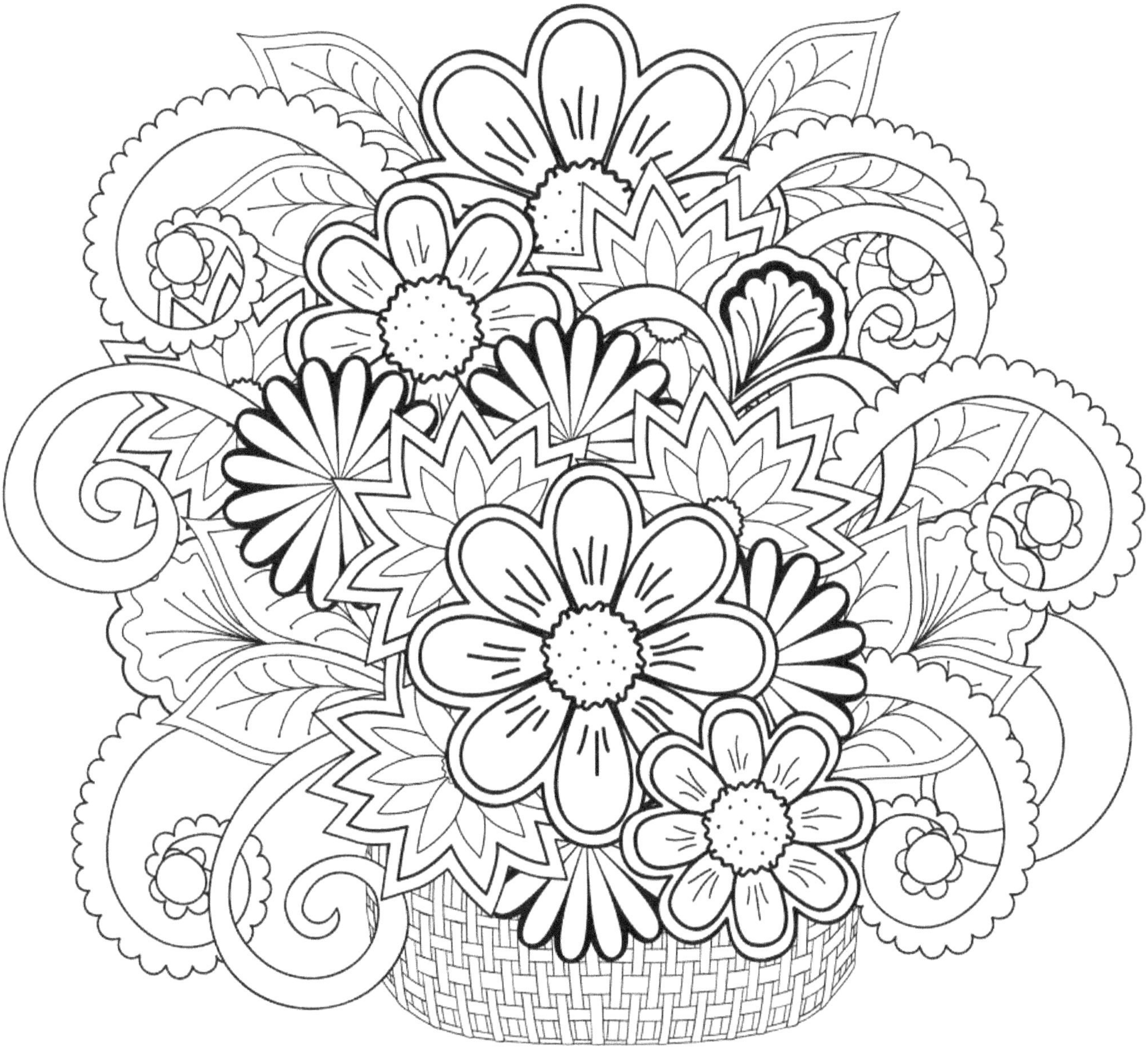

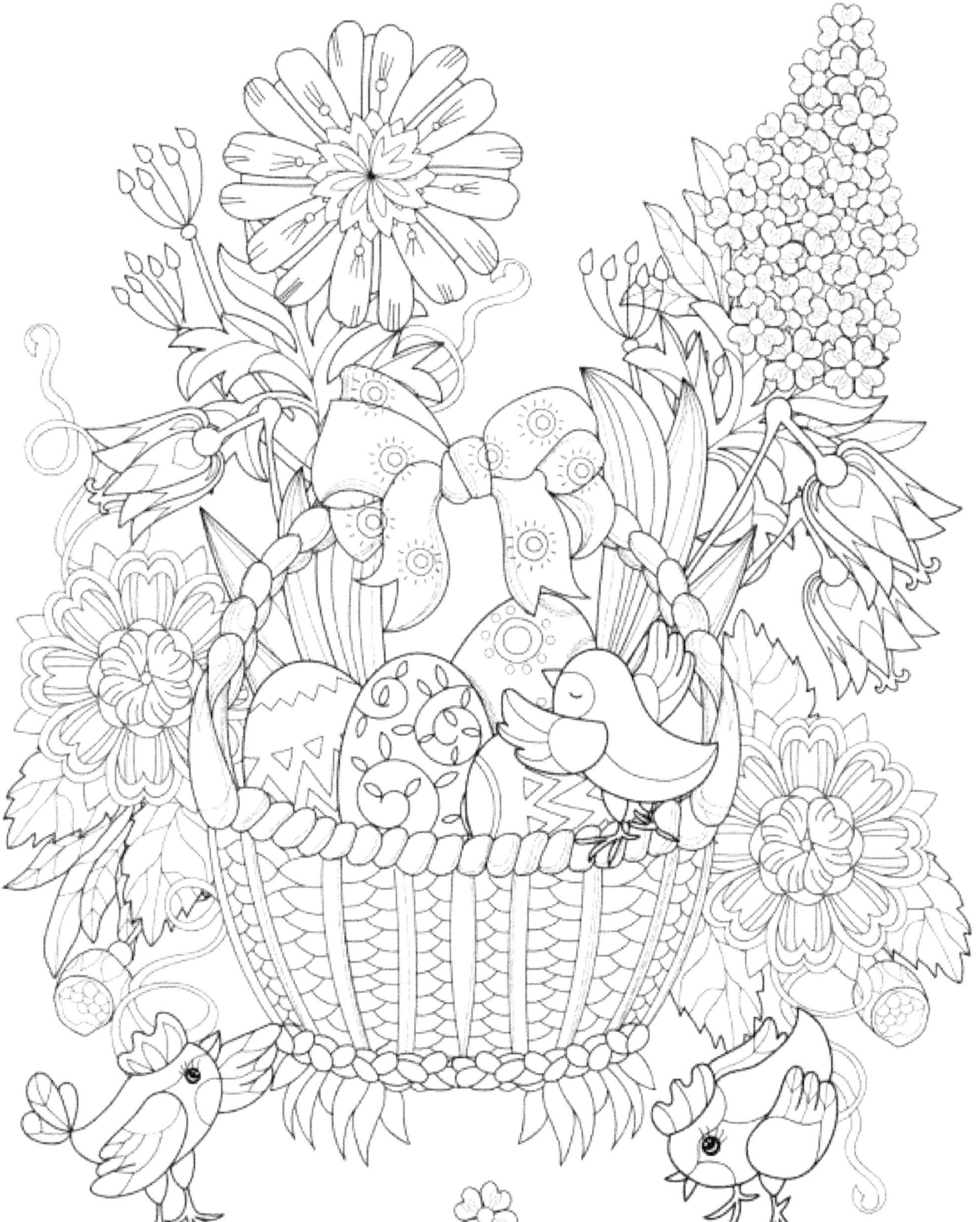

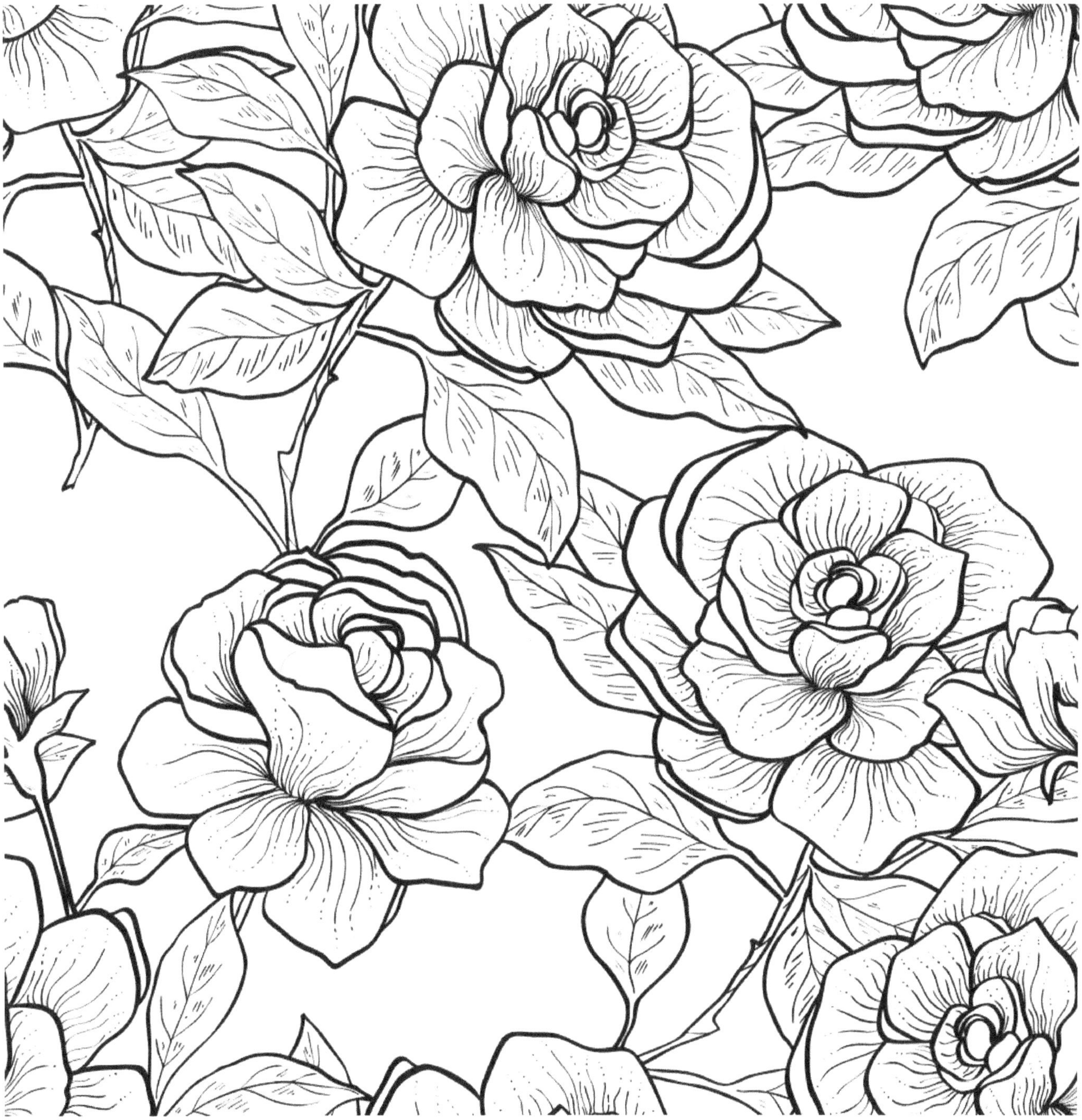

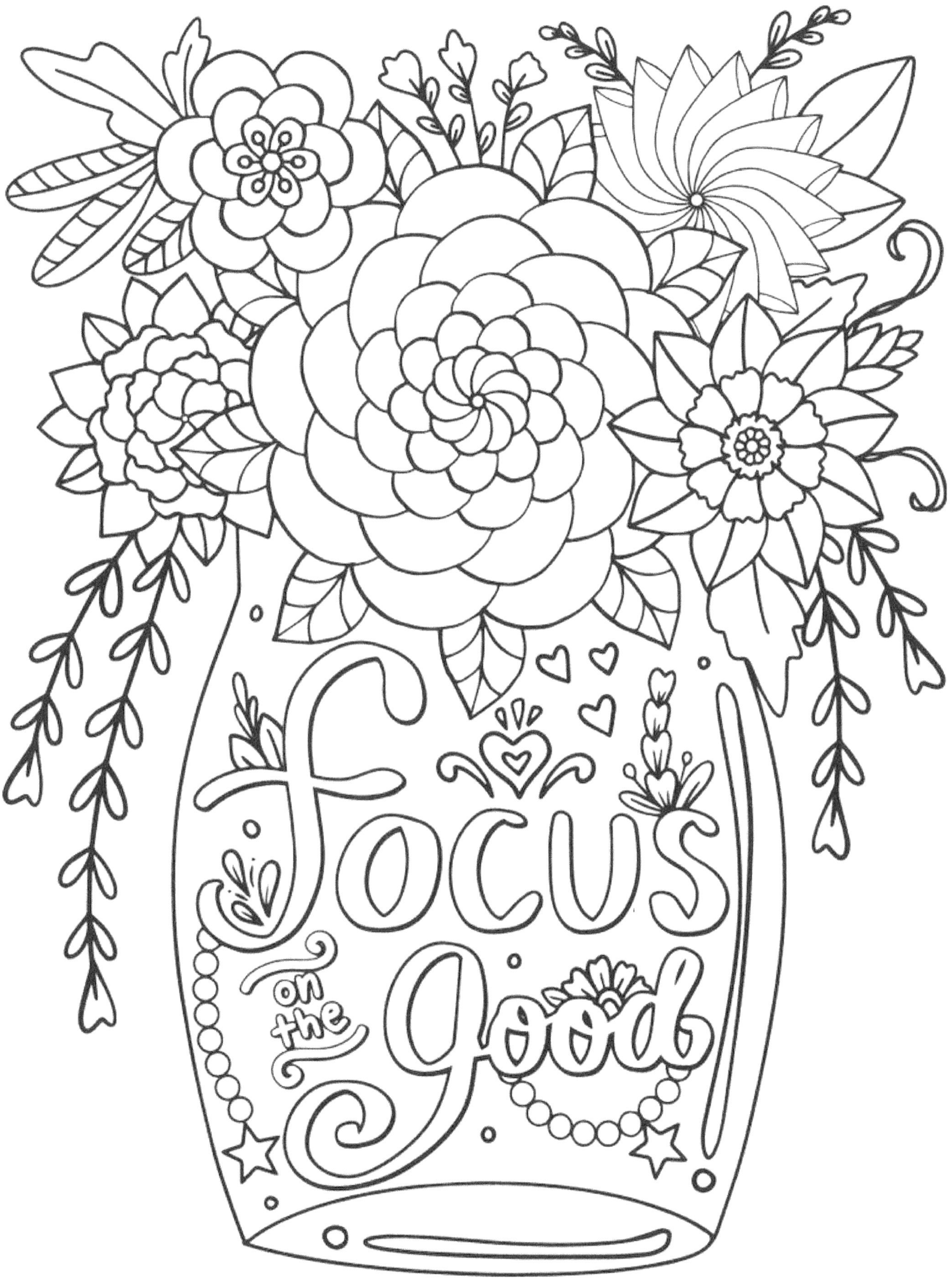
Focus
on the
Good

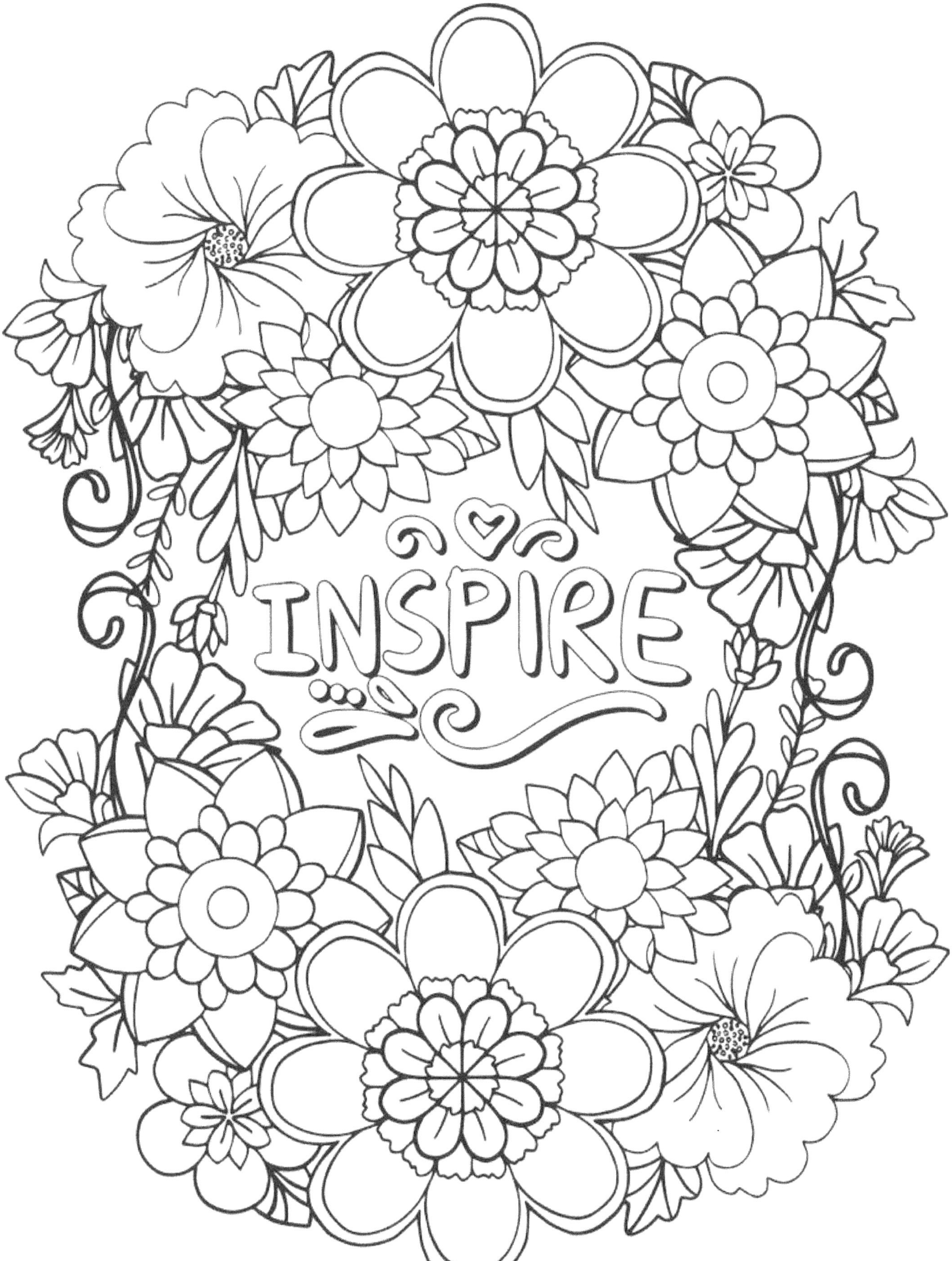
INSPIRE

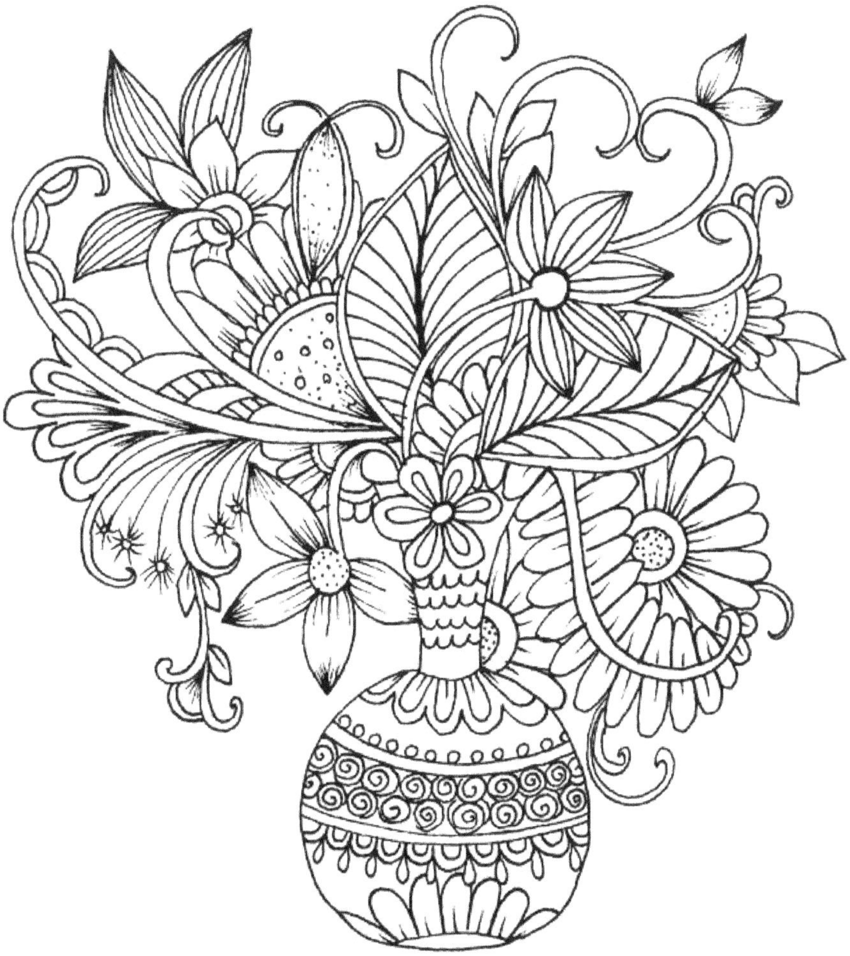

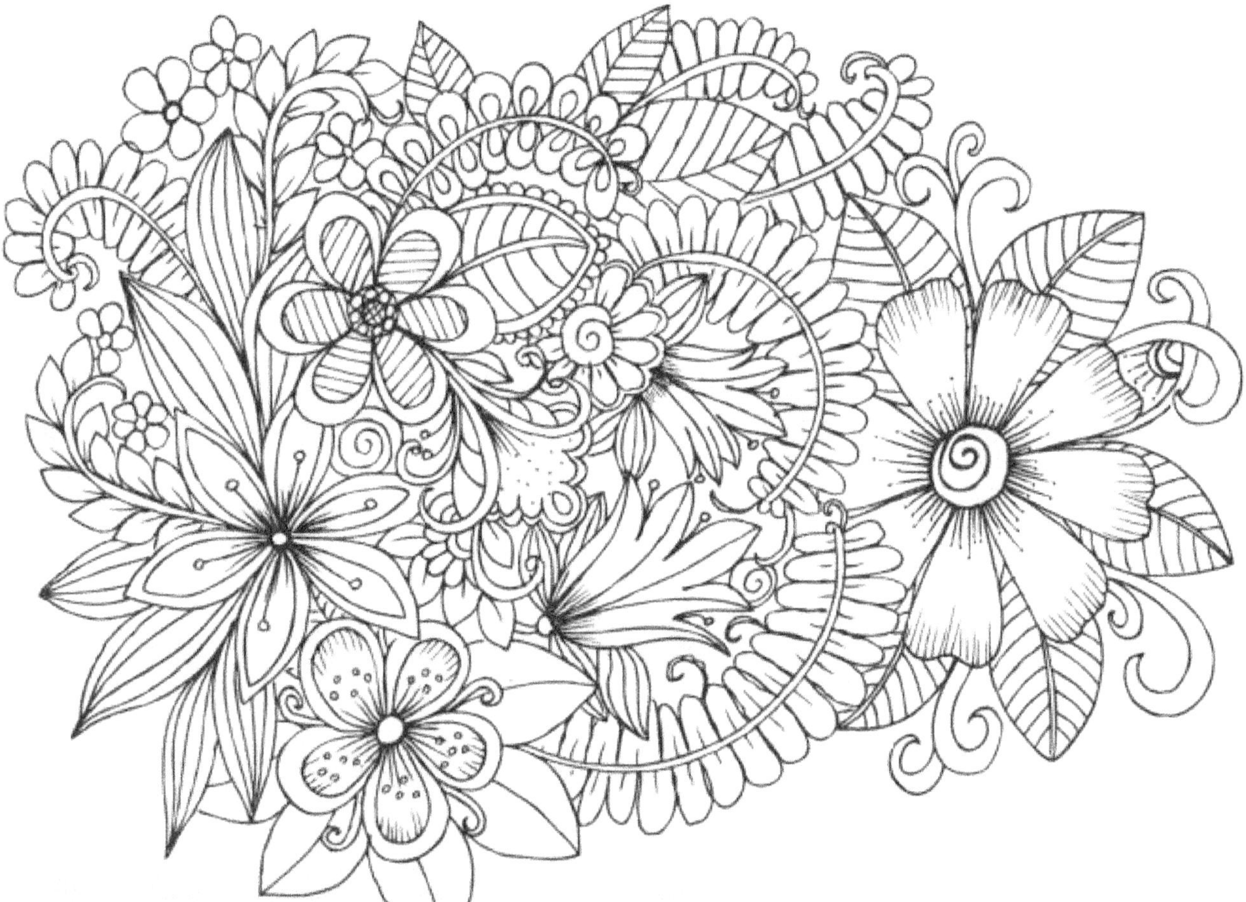

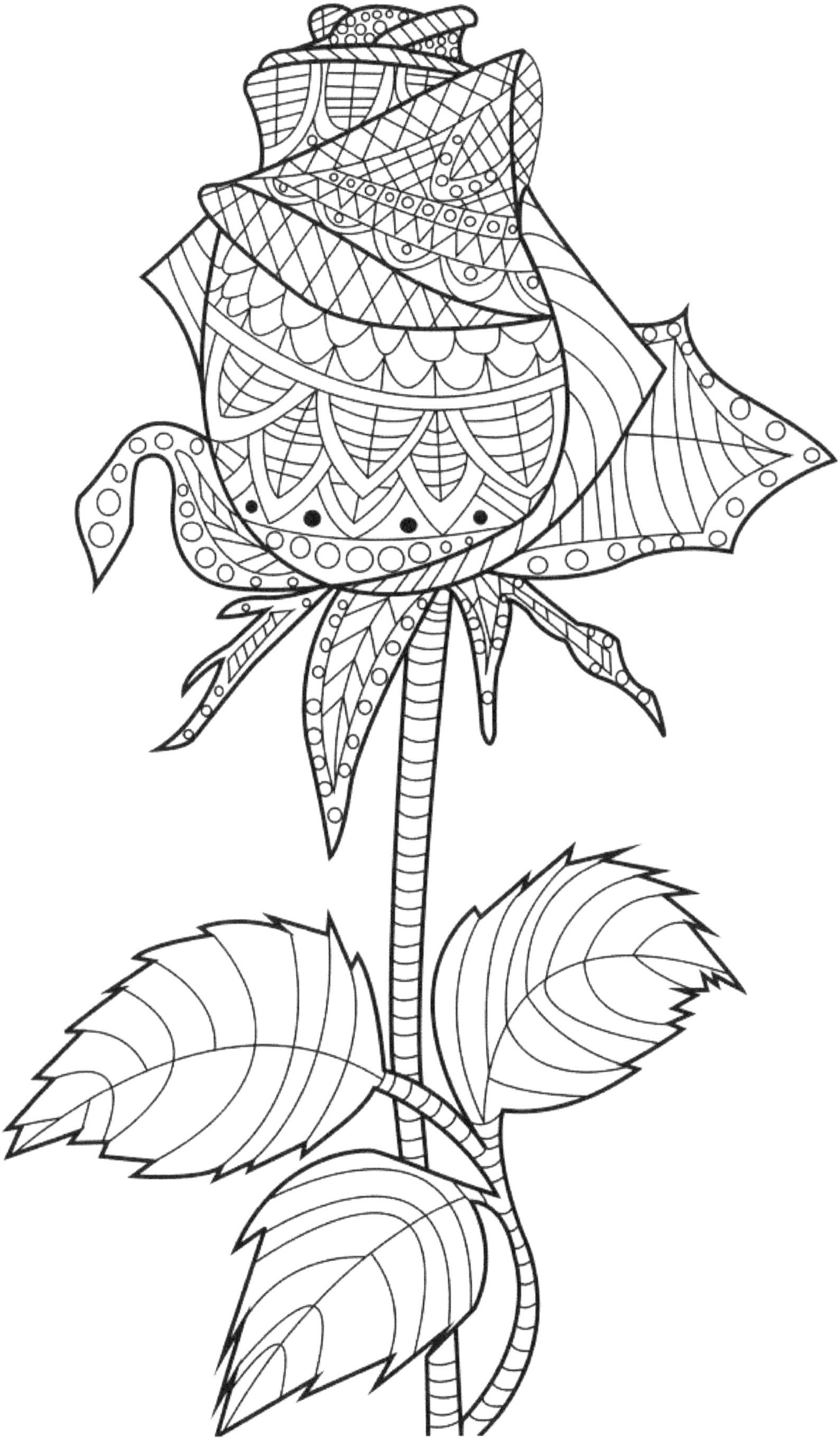

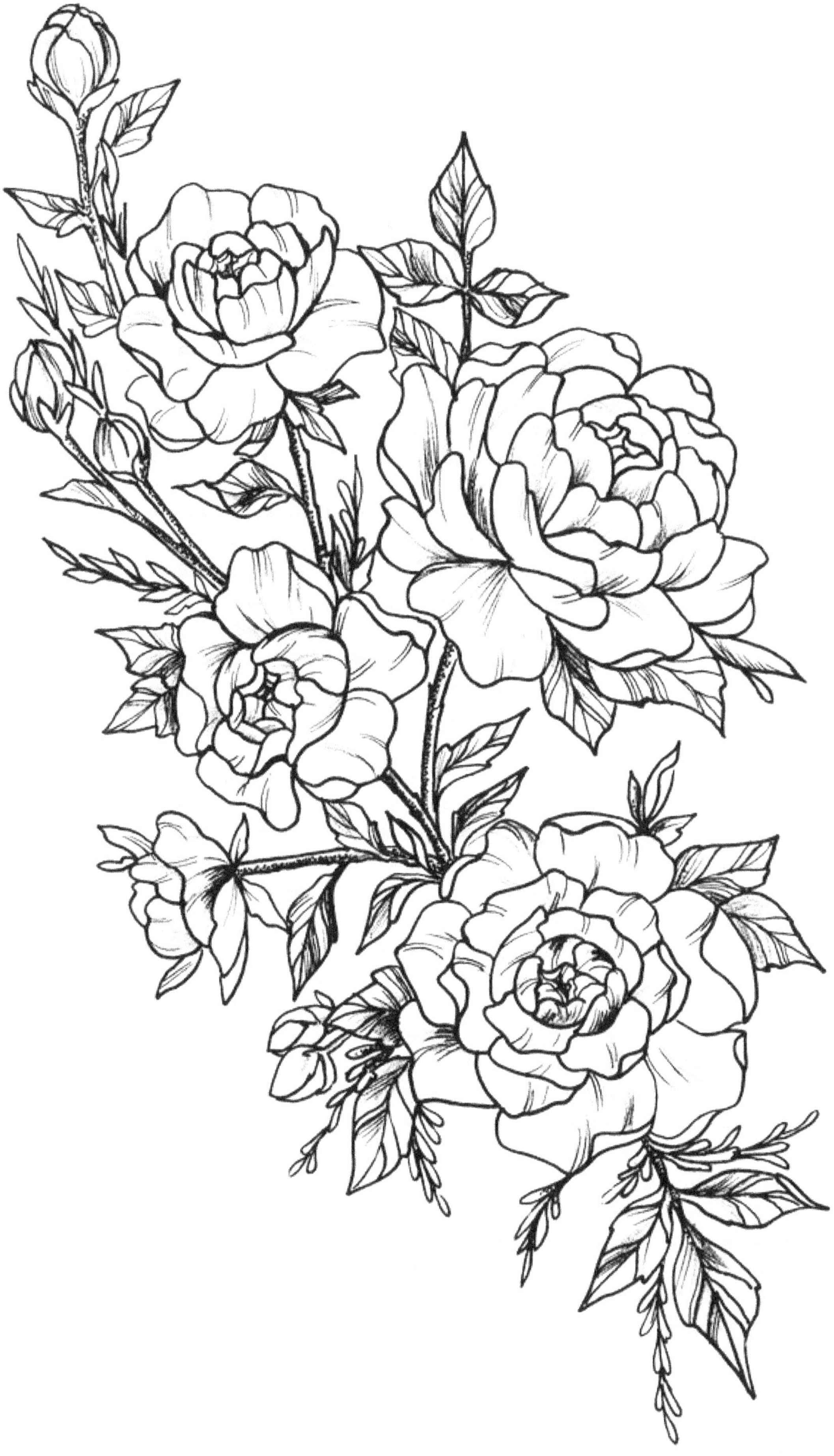

www.ingramcontent.com/pod-product-compliance
Lightning Source LLC
Chambersburg PA
CBHW081524220526
45467CB00010B/3030
9798686077652